Thon

Ulster Sc

Book

By Liam Logan

Photography by Boyd McClurg
Pages: 16,17,18,19,24,25,38,39,50,52,53,58,59,60,74,80,81,83,90,91,
94,95,96,101,114,115,121,133,139,142,143,152,156,157.
Illustrations by Stephen Shaw
Pages: 29,35,37,41,42,43,45,128.
Celine McGlynn/Treasure Each Voice
Teresa Duggan *Page 15*
Gerry Milligan *Page 30/31*
Anne O'Donnell *Page 79*
Neha Shinghal *Page 124*
Mervyn Keys *Cover photo and page 109*
The remaining photography is by the author.

This book is dedicated to Inge, Judy, Angie, Annie, Joe, Hafi, Anwer and Ali.

This project is supported by the
Ministerial Advisory Group (MAG)

Ulster-Scots Academy

Department of
**Culture, Arts
and Leisure**
www.dcalni.gov.uk

Published by Galdanagh Publishing

Printed By Premier Print and Design Ltd.

Foreword

While I assume full responsibility for the words here, I would like to thank Boyd McClurg for his wonderful photography, Stephen Shaw for his illustrations, Celine McGlynn and Treasure Each Voice for their wonderful paintings and Mervyn Keys for his striking cover photograph. They add something special to this book.

While there is no narrative thread, each piece stands alone, there is a link nonetheless. My aim is to try and show that many Ulster Scots words and phrases are a part of everyday speech for many people in Northern Ireland or if you prefer the northern parts of Ireland.

Perhaps you have never met a slabber or a gansh, never footered with something, never had a wee toaty drap o milk in your tay. Many people have and I am grateful for all the kind words from readers who got enjoyment from the columns. Most of us are only one or two generations from the land and while many Ulster Scots words are incorporated into everyday urban speech, there is a rich linguistic tradition associated with rural life which lives on in the minds and the mouths of country dwellers and in the memories of their friends and relatives.

People often ask me if I know this word or that term; "my granny/father/uncle/aunt used that all the time" they'll say. And sometimes I do, many times I don't.

I have a standard piece of advice when the gaps in my knowledge are cruelly exposed; read James Fenton's "The Hamely Tongue", a constant source of pleasure, a work of scholarship and a labour of love by someone who has a deep love of Ulster Scots. I hope this book similarly pleases its readers.

3

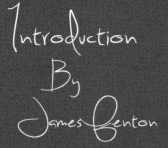

Introduction
By
James Fenton

Liam Logan's 'Thon Ulster Scots Book' is a wide-ranging, comprehensive and authentic guide to the rich figurative speech of that part of County Antrim the author has called "the hame o the Hamely Tongue".

Liam Logan grew up in that area, in Galdanagh, near Ballinaloob (my home townland), Dunloy and Ballymoney.

His delightful exposition is, as it could only be, the work of a native speaker.

He is familiar with the shades of meaning, subtle or blunt, the nuances and the variations of emphasis that can make the same expression serve as a simple comment, a cautionary aside, a word of approval or a total put down.

Each piece centres on the chosen theme, developing and explaining the phrases, sayings and metaphors in which it features.

The style is, as it should be, mostly light-hearted and conversational.

The native speaker, especially the exile (indulging in nostalgia or refurbishing conversational skills), and the reader with little or no knowledge of genuine Ulster Scots will enjoy this generous review of its richness and variety.

I commend it to both.

Preface

In his new book, Liam Logan brings to light the depths and riches of our Ulster-Scots language and culture, our shared identity and the long established links between Ulster and Scotland.

While it may appear to be a light-hearted read, the author's clever use of words and graphics provides an inspired introduction to the linguistic history and traditions of Ulster and Scotland. This volume will be a guaranteed starting place for enthusing young people and educators to look further into this essential part of our shared history with outstanding illustrations demonstrating the beauty of our country.

"Thon Ulster Scots Book" represents a unique learning-tool for all in our community, young and old alike, from different cultural and religious traditions, seeking to know more about our shared history. Above all, as so many people in Northern Ireland strive daily to reach a more peaceful and shared future, this book will be an outstanding resource in learning to live together through sharing our past.

Cecil Linehan. MBE, M.Phil (TCD), FICD, BDS (NUI.), D.ORTH (RCSE).
Co-Founder, All Children Together, the movement for the development of integrated education by consent in Northern Ireland, founded 1972.

January 2014

Preface

Ulster-Scots or "Ullans" is the variety of the Scots language traditionally found in parts of Northern Ireland and Donegal.

I am proud that Liam Logan has decided to publish this intriguing and most interesting introduction to authentic Ulster-Scots. A native speaker from Dunloy, he has been to the forefront in the development and popularisation of the language.

I have known him as a colleague and friend for many years and his wisdom and wit are proverbial.

If you do not read another book on Ulster-Scots, be sure you read this one.

Dr Ian Adamson OBE

Contents

Acknowledgements

I'd like to thank James Fenton for his continuing inspiration, encouragement and good humour, Chris Spurr for his patience and intelligence, Dr Ian Adamson for his unstinting generosity and friendship and Darragh McIntyre for his support and crack. Special thanks to Jon Bleakney, Judith Harper and Margaret Sinnamon for the help and advice.

Particular gratitude goes to Boyd McClurg, Stephen Shaw, Celine McGlynn and the Treasure Each Voice artists, Teresa Duggan, Gerry Milligan, Anne O'Donnell and Neha Shinghal, not forgetting all the folk at Premier Print and Design for all their hard work and artistry.

A Bit O A Druth

One of the great attractions about the Hamely Tongue as James Fenton, the poet and lexicographer, has christened Ulster Scots, is the richness that the tongue gives to everyday speech in Northern Ireland or Ireland or Ulster or whatever your preference happens to be.

When I was younger, the only heat in winter was from peats cut in the summer. Coal was a luxury undreamt of. The work of cutting peats (for which, by the way, one required a Lurgan spade, longer than an ordinary spade, hence the expression 'a face like a Lurgan spade') from the bank and stacking them in castles to dry was an activity always carried out in the moss. Inevitably this distant place was far from potable water, running or otherwise. If you felt a **druth**, and believe me you did (because no matter what the Met Office may tell you, the summers **were** warmer) you could slake it with cold buttermilk. I've shown this delightful drink to my children on a number of occasions but they have reacted with a marked lack of enthusiasm. Actually, they have fled screaming. Indeed, suggestions about imbibing this elixir of the gods have been met with requests for the local social services.

But no matter how refreshing the buttermilk may have been, it was nothing to the heady nectar of cold sweet milky tea drunk from a milk bottle stopped with a clean rag, usually a bit of a Morton's flour bag. I've never even tried to introduce the offspring to this.

That was how I recall **druth** being dealt with. But this wasn't for everyone.

It could be that one of your neighbours (or God forbid, one of your (usually wide) family circle), was known and described as a bit of a **druth**. This indicated his (for it was inevitably a he) preference for a different solution to the problem of thirst, one which involved waters of a stronger nature.

Waters, in fact, of an alcoholic nature. And not always in the moss. Indeed, infrequently in the moss and more often in one of the local hostelries, spartan all male establishments, far removed from the theme pubs of today. Oft times there were other **druthy** individuals present, so, inevitably, he had companionship.

My mother's relationship with **druth** had a lot less to do with liquid refreshment, fortified or otherwise, and much more to do with the weekly wash or more exactly, the drying thereof. A day with a bit of **druth** was a lot more likely to dry the clothes on the line. 'There's great **druth** the day' or more often, given our prevailing climate during most of the year, 'There's not much **druth** the day'.

Though obviously not in the summer.

Size Disnae Metter

Sometimes Ulster Scots takes a perfectly functioning English word and freights it with a set of meanings peculiar to the hamely tongue. When I was wee, all I wanted to be was **big**. Nowadays, if you're **big**, all you want is to be wee.

Big has a number of uses in Ulster Scots, not all of them relating to physical size.

If folk are described as **big people**, this has more to do with their social standing in the community or their possession of adequate financial resources rather than their girth or weight. Although that might also have been the case.

People who have not always seen eye to eye but who have belatedly discovered the concept and joys of brotherly love might well be described as **big** and those who aren't just as chummy might be identified as **no big** or perhaps **no as big as they wur**, possibly indicating a contretemps.

Rotundity or corpulence in general is not necessarily being referred to if an individual is described as **big o the erse** (although it's a possibility). Rather the person being described is clumsy or awkward. Although it's hard to deny that the description **an erse that big ye could clod a britchin ower it** (of a generously proportioned individual, usually female, a vivid phrase for which I am indebted to Sam Agnew of Kilwaughter) employs big in the conventional English sense.

While not strictly relevant, I am reminded of my brother's experience many years ago as a young producer for BBC Scotland. He was working on the development of

a strand of programming for the Scots Gallic language (sometimes known as Erse, itself a mispronunciation of Irish) particularly targeted on speakers who had a basic knowledge of Scots Gallic but who were returning to the language after an absence, either linguistic or geographic. The working title of the programme, 'Brush Up Your Erse', sadly didn't make it to air.

Big o the mooth or **big o the gub** indicates someone with a loose tongue, one who might be deemed as unable 'to houl their ain watter'. **Big o' the heid** doesn't imply possession of an over inflated sense of your own worth but rather a stupid person; thus **'big o' the heid'** clearly indicates **'small of the brain'**.

An unexpected turn of events might be described as a **'big yin'** and empty boasting could be labelled **'big tak'**.

Aberrant or antisocial behaviour (or indeed the day to day strains of family life, according some mothers) might result in a stay at the **'Big Hoose'**, a destination which varied according to your location. In County Antrim, Hollywell, in County Down, Downpatrick; Belfast had Purdysburn and in Derry it was Gransha. My mother in law hails from Dungannon and my wife assures me on bad days she threatened to end her days in Omagh.

If something were to be described as **'big odds'**, this doesn't indicate a potentially hefty payout from Barney Eastwood or Alfie McLean but rather denotes something important but usually expressed in a sarcastic or ironic way. A 'big deal' in English means something important but if someone says 'Big deal' it usually means 'No big deal'. So is it also in Ulster Scots, **nay big odds**.

Gye Rugh

When I come to pen a piece, I aye hae *'rugh idea whit I'd dae'*. Equating on many levels with 'rough', *'rugh'* still has a distinct meaning, peculiar to Ulster Scots.

To describe your (perhaps temporary or holiday) lodgings as **'rugh enugh'** is to indicate a slightly sub standard state of affairs. The same critique applied to a neighbour's house is an altogether more damning indictment. The modifier is vitally important. *'Gye rugh'* is worse again and if your living quarters are in a state of total dereliction, they might be described as being *'rugh as a badger's erse'*.

If an individual were to lose their composure or allow their exuberance to get the better of them, it might be said that they were **'cuttin up rugh'**. And if the person were possessed of a slovenly nature or an unkempt appearance, they might also be classified as *'rugh'*.

I have heard those hardy Ulster Scots souls who take ship across the sheugh to Scotland in pursuit of their favourite football teams describe the crossing as '*brave an rugh*' or '*as rugh as I hay seen it*'. For the veterans, inevitably perhaps, it's nearly always '*no as rugh as I hay seen it*'. Grub prepared to a standard well below that of Cordon Bleu and in circumstances evidencing a healthy disregard for environmental health food safety regulations might be deemed '*rugh packin*'. To slightly paraphrase Fenton, '*Ye'd need to be mair nor hungry tae face what was put up tae ye*'. This, of course, would never happen on the ferry to Scotland. '*Rughie*', sometimes called '*roozle*', is bread baked from oatmeal, flour and cold boiled 'prootas' (the noble spud).

A '*rughness*' of money indicates a not insubstantial (or indeed a considerable) amount of coin. A young woman might be made more marriageable if the putative match were to include a '*rughness o money*'. Such an individual might be said to '*hay a guid purse tae her erse*'. If a task were to be partially done but in large measure completed, it might be said that the '*rugh o its daen*'.

Like this piece, since no work of art is ever completed, merely abandoned…….

Tales O Heids

Rather than focus on one single word, I'm going to concentrate on a part of the body. The '**heid**', perched atop '**yer shoothers**', is recognised as the seat of reason. Or perhaps more frequently, as the seat of unreason. An individual attracting the description '**aff yer heid**' or indeed '**awa in the heid**' might have been brought to this pass by a situation or a person who might very well '**pit ye wrang in the heid**'. This may also have the result of identifying you as a '**heidcase**' or a '**madheid**'. Or perhaps evidenced that you had suffered a bout of the '**heid staggers**'.

Hunger was not a factor if somebody '**ate the heid aff ye**' rather a verbal exchange of a pointed nature was indicated. This might also be rendered as '**ate the face aff**' or indeed '**ate the bake aff**' but more of this later. All the foregoing could result in you getting '**yer heid in yer han**'.

If a matter was deemed to be '**ower the heid o**', this was not to suggest that an overly intellectual argument was beyond the grasp of an interlocutor but that the present circumstances has arisen due to this particular cause. Those who propose an unwise or irrational course of action or adopt a stance, which could reasonably be called unreasonable, might attract the comment '**yer heid's cut**', but not in a way that requires bandages. People lacking any modicum of shame, modesty or tact would oft times be asked '**hae ye nae skin on yer face**' and a smiling hypocrite might be named '**oul fair-face**'. If a young man were to ask a young lady to a social engagement as part of a courtship ritual, he (or indeed, she) could be said to be '**facing**' a girl (or a boy).

If you '**gether the broos**', you make a scowl or a frown. Your '**ee**' or perhaps more accurately, your '**een**', are not only a window on the soul but could be used for the production of crocodile tears drawing the comment '**yer blether's near yer een**'. Accidental or deliberate observational failures could be ascribed to an individual being '**blin o an ee**'.

Ears are 'lugs' and were most often employed as a disciplinary adjunct, as in 'a clash on the lug'.

The '**mooth**' or the '**bake**', the mouth, also had physical force references such as '**a slap in the mooth**', usually resulting from a predilection for '**takkin when ye should hae bin listenin**'. Such uncouth folk might be asked to '**shut their bake**' or indeed, more politely, '**howl their wheesht**' before they passed a remark they might live to regret and had to '**tak oot wi yer teeth what ye put in wi yer tongue**'. The selfish and greedy might be in danger of '**takin the bite oot o yer mooth**' in their anxiety to sate their own appetites, even if the tiny morsel were only sufficient to '**taste yer mooth**'. And if the food were sufficiently tasty to provoke excess salivation, the overflow might be said to be '**rinnin doon the weeks o yer mooth**'.

But not in polite company. Unless you had '**nae skin on yer face**'.

Less is Mair

I'd like to give some consideration to the vexed and vexing question of measurement in Ulster Scots, not only quantity or distance but also, perhaps, intensity or numeric values.

'**Bit**' would be the generic term (*a bit o rain, a bit o meat*) for quantity but not an exact measure (*"a bit o a barney"*). '**A drap**' or '**a taste**' can usually be easily interchanged but is generally, but not exclusively, applied to liquid measures *("A wee drap o tay" "A drap o learnin's aisy carriet" "The country's crying oot for a taste o rain")*; admittedly, the last remark is not heard all that frequently.

If you leave to one side expressions like *"whut wud drap aff the blak o yer nail"*, a term of metaphorical quantity (or lack thereof) rather than scientific measurement, I'd guess the smallest (conversationally) measurable amount to be '**a wee toaty bit**',

(*"A jist tak a wee toaty bit o milk in ma tay"*) obviously leading to '**a wee bit**'. (*"It's only a wee bit further on"*) but this might also be employed as an understatement *"Thon boy's a wee bit wile"* to perhaps convey the presence of rather more '*wile*' than might be acceptable in polite society.

Then comes '**a brave wee bit**' (*"He wusnay drunk but he had tane a brave wee bit"*) though again, without independent scientific verification, the only real measurement is comparative, this being a lesser amount than '**a brave bit**'. (*"I didnay see the hale thing but A seen a brave bit"*).

The term '**big bit**' to my mind carried the meaning - the most of, what little remained was, to the speaker, of little moment. (*"It's nay use comin noo when the big bit o it's dane"*).

Numbers are often communicated in a similarly inexact fashion but there would be some general agreement as to their ranking. '**A wheen**' would be '*mare nor yin or two*' bit no as mony as a brave wheen'. Slightly larger again is '**a gether up**' but on occasion this term was applied to indicate a group whose provenance or antecedents were of questionable pedigree, that the quality of the quantity was somewhat below standard (*"**I went alang but thur wuz only a gether up o thim**"*).

In the same vein is '**a clatchin**', a derogatory term for a group or collection of people or things (*"**There wuz a clatchin o gulpins ootside the pub**"*).

Then might come '**a clatter**' meaning a large number (*"**We wur jist sittin doon when a clatter o her yins landed**"*).

'**A lock**' would also be a considerable amount of similar (or possibly slightly greater) value than "**a clatter**'. There would be fairly wide interpretations with variations bearing, to some extent, on the nature of the matter under discussion; *"**A lock o yins wudnay hay him aboot thim but he hiz din nathin tay me**"* almost certainly denotes a different numerical value to that indicated by '***Me and him went oot an got a lock o drink**'* but it is nevertheless an expression of some numerical significance; the first quantifies people while the second counts bottles and halfuns.

Carrying no agreed numerical values, '**a tear**' would outrank '**a lock**'; I think I would regard the greater drunkard as he who had *"**tane a tear o drink**"* rather than he who had *"**tane a lock o drink**"* although indubitably both could be referred to as having had '*a feed o drink*' again, a term of significant quantity. Perhaps conveying that the capacity of our two imagined topers (of whatever magnitude) had been reached, they might be deemed by some to be '**full**' (*"**As full as a po**" "**As full as forty cats**" "**As full as the eye o a pick**"*) sometimes rendered as '**foo**'.

The topics of time and money will require mair discussion anither time.

Stannin

In the context of our electoral system, I thought I'd like to consider character assessment in the Tongue, given that there is so much of it at the doorsteps and on our radios and televisions during elections. Or perhaps that should be character assassination?

As I have noted before, the Tongue tends to have a slightly (in fact, a considerably) larger vocabulary which can be applied for uncharitable purposes, there being many more words employable in the service of criticism rather than praise. I would emphasise that this is not meant necessarily as a comment on the quality of our prospective tribunes of the people.

Candidates who might be expected to defend their various points of view vigorously or loudly may be said to have a tendency to "**argy doon yer throat**".

And if an individual presents themselves on the hustings while not completely sharing the prevalent social mores of the constituency or ward, they might draw the remark "**it's a wunther thon boy's allooed oot at a**".

Occasionally, the granite bulwarks of the democratic process allow through an individual who might charitably be characterised as less than a rock of dependability, "**He'll let ye doon, as sure as gun's iron**".

There are a rare instances where a not wholly trustworthy individual has a hand in political matters "**He'll niver say ocht tae yer face, but he'll wheetle an tak ahintbaks**", but luckily, we have none of these scallywags anywhere within our processes.

The political life isn't one that allows for the long quiet evenings by "**yir ane fire**". The prospective politician is "**Aye awa wae himsel (or**

hersel) tae a nighber hoose ivery nicht". It might be thought that the activity of the politician was making little contribution to the further advancement of the human race particularly when they are perceived to be "**stannin wae the twa airms the yin length**".

The obverse to the elector's perspective is that of the candidate. The campaign not only allows the candidate to press his or her case to the citizen for elective office, it also affords the citizen a rare opportunity to directly interrogate those who would rule the jurisdiction.

I have it on good authority from an independent and, obviously, unnamed political source that following a rather heated contretemps on the campaign trail an individual voter who had been dissatisfied with their candidate's policies was described by the candidate, albeit sotto voce, as being "**as akward a man as iver chowed cheese**".

A cruel and mischievous untruth has been perpetrated on the public giving rise to accusations that politicians are selfish individuals, only interested in "**linin' their ane poakets**"

"**Aye takkin frae an niver putting tae**".

Putative politicians should bear in mind the Ulster-Scots rendition of the old saw "**life is tough and then you die**":

"**It's al uphill an agane the wun**"

On the Road Again

It wasn't necessary to be familiar with black American street slang to understand the import of the song "Hit the Road, Jack" by the late great Ray Charles. We all knew what he had to do.

"Road" has a range of meanings in Ulster Scots and I'd like to explore a few of them today. Before exploring this road, less travelled recently, it might be worth mentioning that there subtleties to the English meaning of road. A main road is inevitably referred to as a line (*the Ballymena Line, the Rasharkin Line*) but even a rough track across a bog (*boag*) would have been called "*the moss road*". I was reared *(raired)* on a road that rejoiced in the name "*the sunk road*", so christened due to its propensity to flooding in bad weather. (Yes there was the odd bit of rain in my youth, whiles).

A road man or surface man was a worker dedicated to the upkeep of the Queens highway and its attendant ditches, gulleys, verges and drains.

Before crossing the road, it was and is always advisable to "*aye luck baith roads before stepping oot*") and on the road , it is essential to "*keep her between the hedges*".

There was the metaphoric road of life and the *cri de couer* of the veteran about its unfairness and fundamental inequality (*the oul doag for the hard road and the pup for the pad*) when the tough tasks are entrusted to someone with experience while the simple jobs are left to the novice.

It can mean distance (*he's fit tay hit the ba a lang road*, occasionally heard of a golfer) as well as admission charge (*we had tay pi wur ain road in*). A series of misdemeanours or incompetences in one's place of employment might result in the sack or "*getting the road*".

If a colleague or a competitor was unworthy of comparison with your own abilities or talents, you might be moved to comment that "*you wudnay see them in yer road*". You might well encourage such a person to "get oot o me road" as their very presence may be unhelpful, either practically or otherwise. If a personal relationship had deteriorated to the point of indifference or even outright hostility, a person might "*niver luck the road ye wur oan*". If a job were left incomplete, it might be said to be "half roads done" or done incompetently might be "done half roads".

A location could be handy ("*on yer road hame*" "*on yer road by*") or it might not be handy ("*oot o yer road*" "*I could niver live in a place as ooty ther road as thon*"). The deviation could be metaphorical as well ("*he wud go ooty his road tay day ye a guid turn*" or "*he wud go ooty his road tay day ye a bad turn*" not so common, I think)

The price of a good, if within the bounds of normal commercial mores can be said to be " *no ooty the road*".

Far Oot Man

The other night on television I watched a film and one of the characters remarks to another "Far out, man, far out" and it reminded me of the first time I heard this expression which is, of course, based on an Ulster Scots phrase. But more of that later.

"**Oot**" has a number of meanings and applications in Ulster Scots. At its simplest, it is a rendition of "out". If an individual is "**oot for themsels**", they tend to pursue a selfish agenda. This could, in turn, lead to a deterioration in personal relationships better known as an "**ootfa**"; this might lead to people "**drinkin the bit oot**" or "**fechtin the bit oot**". Or indeed both. Such behaviour might be described as "**ooty a raison**". Anyplace outside the home, either specific locations or generally out of doors, could be described as "**ootby**" and a piece of land or a farm separated from the "**hame place**" by some distance might be referred to as an "**oot-fairm**" or "**ootlyin fairm**". If such a farm was close to a particular locale but not in it, this might be identified as "**ootside o Rasharkin**".

Extravagant or exorbitant prices or demands were "**ooty the wie**" however if you were out of practice, a bit rusty or had lost the habit of an activity, you might be "**oot o the wie o**".

Younger men and women poised at the front door, anxious for the society of others and dressed accordingly, were "**ready for oot**".

Which, in a way, brings me back to the film. I must have been "**oot**" at a wake or a gathering of some description, maybe a guest tea. The gathering was having a yarn about a local gentleman, one of those individuals who annoy the older generation but exert a strange fascination for the younger generation, myself included. He didn't work, at least not the way other folk did, but he seemed to pass the time agreeably enough although his dress sense was somewhat unconventional, to say the least. One might have described him as *outré*.

If anybody adopted an unusual dress code in our corner of North Antrim, people said he was like Hashter Gammle, a man of the roads not noted for his sartorial elegance. Oddly enough, this particular gentleman was always brave and popular with the women. Perhaps he appealed to their nurturing side.

Anyway, the conversation at the gathering came to be concerned with this chap and his personal life and habits; truth to tell it was more of a critique, what would be referred to as a "**reddin' up o the pedigrees**".

But there was one man in the company who was a kind of a relative of our sartorially challenged subject and somebody said "**Is he no a freen o yours, John**" (in other words "Are you not a relative of that fellow, John?") and John turns round and says "**Far oot, man, far oot**"

A Brave Face

Let's face it, most of the Ulster Scots meanings for the word "**face**" are shared with English but we'll try and keep a "**guid face**" on matters linguistic.

Of course there has to be a sense of the word that relates to the cutting of peats, what I like to think of as the signature activity of not only the Ulster Scots but also the Irish and the Scots. The front or "**breesht**" of a peat bank i.e. that part of the "**boag**" or "**moss**" from whence peats were cut, was referred to as the "**face**".

Another common meaning for "**face**" would be the cutting or trimming of the side of a hedge, often accomplished with the use of a "**slasher**", on occasion, a "**bull hook**".

If a business was failing, it might have been described as "**no bein' fit tay wash its face**" although this carried no implications or inferences about the personal habits or hygiene of the proprietors or employees.

There is no shared understanding with English of the use of "**face**" to mean court, not the venue where the law is dispensed or a royal palace or entourage or indeed a tennis, volleyball, basketball or squash playing area, but rather in the sense of paying court, having a romantic relationship with someone that you hope to marry.
Or at least with someone you want to know better than you do at present.

It might mean asking someone out on a date or to go for a walk or to take a breath of air outside a dancehall. Most importantly, it was never used in conversation with the object of your affections rather it was employed when conversing with third parties ("**Are you for facin her the morrow?**" "**A'm gan tay face him nay metter what onybody says**")

Not every bit of "**courtin' in the kitchen**" led to an encounter with the clergy or the Registrar or indeed an irate father. However, this latter, if and when encountered, might have been inclined to "**pit on a face**" (look not best pleased) and **mair nor yin o the wans** I come across tried to "**ate the face aff me**", something completely different from what I had been trying to accomplish with my new friend although the description may conjure an image which might have borne a passing resemblance to our activities.

I have whiles been accused of "**hayin' nae skin on my face**" for such impudence but at least I had the good grace "**tay get a rid face**". As did my co-conspirators, on those occasions when someone had been able to "**gie them a rid face**".

Violent fathers and indeed, violent spouses, when their blood was stirred, were in danger of "**knockin' the face aff ye**", "**chowin' the face aff ye**" or "**batin' the face aff ye**" if you were discovered "**in flagrante delicto**" (literally, while the crime is blazing, but in Latin rather than Ulster Scots). Overindulgence in "**courtin'** " or frequent detection by prying eyes and subsequent chastisement might result in a boady "**gan aff the face o' the earth**" or failing in health and undergoing dramatic and drastic weight loss, a sort of Ulster Scots alternative to the Atkins Diet.

Of course the fates have their own special way of punishing those men who inappropriately overindulge in the rituals of courtship during their youth and it is a sentence that results in sleep loss, poverty, high blood pressure and constant worry. When these poor unfortunates accede to the state of parenthood, fate sends them daughters. Maybe it's karma.

I have it on good authority that the first twenty-five years are the worst.

Simply the Best

Of coorse he was the Belfast Boy but he was appreciated and loved all ower the world. George was yin o wur ain an he'll be gyley missed. There hays been a lock o words writ an spoke aboot the boy but nane writ in oor ain tongue.

Till noo.

He wus a very dacent boadie wi nay bak dorrs, a good man without devious motives. A wee bit o a drooth, I'll grant ye, but there's nay shortage o them that taks a drap in oor ain wee country. The pitches he played on were slunky an wat, ye might call them a slarry, a wet mess, but he skited ower the grun laik a ballet dancer with defenders in his wake laik a pack o grulshes, slow, awkward and overweight people. George didn't footer aboot because if he had, those defenders he took such joy in humiliating would have gin him a dunt he wudnae forget. They couldnae catch the houl o him, thank goodness. George made them look like they had no footballing abilities or skills whatsoever, resembling nothing so much as an owl wumman wae a stray erse.

People liked him, people even loved him even
though he had his fair share of critics,
nyaffs an nyirs nyitterin at him that
bad it wud gae ye the nyirps;
small insignificant persons,
objectionable niggling little
people, complaining non-stop
in a peevish manner to the
extent that it would make
you fretful, exasperate you or
get on your nerves. To those
critics I would say that they
know as much about football
as my erse knows aboot snipe
shootin.

And he was fond o the lassies; merrried
twice to strikingly beautiful women of whom
it could not be said "Ye wudnae merry hir if the
sovereigns wuz hingin frae hir" rather the sort of blondes who
would "make a bishop kick a hole in a stained glass window" as Raymond
Chandler so eloquently put it. But there was a brave bit o coortin as weel.
It's naw a crime yet an some folk are mair nor a wee bit jealous.

We will mine him for his fitba, his film star good looks, the guid memories he
gin us, the wie he made us a proud. I mine stannin in a lay-by, somewhere
in the mountains between Italy and France back in the 1990s and meeting
a trio of Argentinians who spoke no English (niver mine Ulster Scots) and I
had (and continue to have) no Spanish.

I told them, as best I could, that I came from Belfast (not strictly true
but I was sure they hadn't heard of Dunloy) and they immediately,
instantaneously said "George Best" even though his peak had been many
years before. He made an impact on the world far beyond this wee island. I
think we are all deeply grateful to have walked the earth when he was in his
pomp. I feel laik yin o they defenders he made sport o. He's there in front
o ye, there in front o ye an ye can see him the Best an then he's aff an ye
dinnae know whur he went an ye'r stannin there thinkin "Where'd he go?
Where'd he go?"

Daein a Do

I am indebted to yin o me oul freens, a boadie originally frae jist ootside o Dunloy, a wee toonlan ca'ed Ballymacaldrick, a man by the name o Aidan Dougan.

He e-mailed me recently and toul me o an exchange he had in the late 1970s at a roadside checkpoint, one that neatly illustrates how the word "do" does not always require rendition as "dae", as might be thought by the unwary, an Ulster Scots equivalent of what the English, when referring to French, have called a "faux amis", false friends. The French and English language have hundreds of words which look and/or are pronounced alike in the two languages, including true (similar meanings), false (different meanings), and semi-false (some similar and some different meanings). Unsurprising given their shared romantic roots. So is it also with Ulster Scots and English. Anyway, back to the Seventies.

Brother Dougan pursued gainful employment as a spinner of discs, a DJ, providing entertainment at a wide range of functions including weddings, birthday parties and bar mitzvahs.

En route to one such event somewhere in North or Mid Antrim, he encountered, as many did in that decade, a security checkpoint manned by a local troop of the UDR, the Ulster Defence Regiment; for younger readers, a group of part-time soldiers drawn from the local area.

After an inspection of the vehicle revealed various record decks, microphones and disco lights, one of the soldiers enquired of Bro. Dougan:

"Were ye daein a do?" drawing the response

"Naw, Ah'm gan tae dae a do but if ye dinnae let me gon, Ah'll be daein nae do the night".

"Ye better gon then. Such 'er on". And off he went to dispense his disco wares to a waiting throng gathered at some hostelry.

"Dae" is of course "do" but "do", in common with English, can mean a party, a reception, a "getherin" o some description and this was the case in this exchange. There is also the meaning of swindle ("**He wud dae ye tae the oxters**", one might take advantage of your trusting nature).

Some folk will be familiar with individual who finds the decision making process problematic, who might be described as "daeless". Bad as this affliction may be, worse again is the "boady" who promises much but ultimately delivers little or "naethin", Such a person might be labelled as being " al say an nae dae".

And of coorse, there is "daen", indicating someone or something as being worn out with age or use ("an oul daen man"). Or tiredness ("A cannae dae anither turn for A'm clean daen"). "Daen" can also indicate the completion of a task.

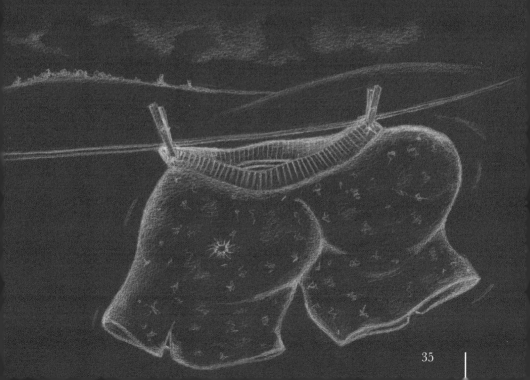

Prootas

At the heart of life in all parts of the country was a relative newcomer to these shores, an import from the Americas named the potato but rendered locally as the "**proota**". In these low carb times, with the farmer diversifying or setting aside and the chip an endangered species (almost), the spud has declined in importance but once it ruled. "**Naw a meal withoot a proota**" is a damning indictment of a poor quality kitchen or insufficient hospitality and the search was always for the "**dry proota**", that holy grail of the Ulster Scots culinary arts. And while modern folk say "**potato bread**", we didn't say "**proota bread**", it was always "**fadge**". The addition of a little oatmeal to the recipe created "**proota oaten**" or "**roozle**".

But whatever part "**prootas**" had on the bill of fare (and it was extensive), the "**getherin o the prootas**" was **gye** hard work. If memory serves, there was a school holiday designated explicitly for "**proota getherin**" though if, as I've heard, the design of the entire school year relates to the agricultural economy's need for cheap or free labour, this should not be too surprising.

"**Liftin prootas**" was a communal activity, often involving family, neighbours and friends and if cash money was part of the deal, it rewarded the worker spectacularly, or so it seemed at the time. Someone, perhaps the owner of the "**prootas**", (**who micht be different boady frae the yin that owned the lan or grun**), kept a note of the bags filled by each "**getherer**" and pay or "**pie**" was by the bag "**gethered**". "**Ye aye kep a good coont yersel**".

"**Prootas was gethered**" in a "**proota basket**", a container shaped like a small cot, and full baskets were emptied into your bag. "**The quicker, the more, the richer**" was the logic but the ache in the back (and I can feel it now this instant, "**mair years later than I care tae mine**") and the coul o your fingers and the blisters on your hands and your "**welton boots**" made welts on your bare legs; it was a hard earned fortune. It's funny how you remember the good times.

The bags were about a hundredweight, eight stone; Lord knows what that is in kilograms but well beyond the lifting powers of the pre-teen in any measurement system. These bags were delivered to the "**proota chute**", a machine that always called to my mind the contraptions employed by Hollywood's gold prospectors to sift out their gold. The "**proota chute**", a sloping wooden structure down which the "**prootas**" poured and the sorters sorted, or "**waaled**" and packed into other bags. I suppose we were prospecting for some sort of gold but this process only for "**prootas gan oot**", "**yins for wur ain pot**" were "**pit in the proota pit**", a grave-shaped pile of "**prootas**" covered with soil, a storage method which worked pretty effectively against all but the hardest of frosts.

Daenae Tak it Thick

As I have indicated on previous occasions, there are a number of words where our local usage coincides in the main with the use in standard English. There are also a number of words, those with more than one (*mair nor yin* or *wan*) usage or meaning, where we share *a wheen o* the meanings but *naw al*. The day I'd like to look at *"thick"*.

The most common application in standard English is as a measurement or estimation of density and this usage is shared with Ulster Scots. ("*The fog was wile thick ower the bak o the mountain*"). There is also a common usage in relation to size ("*She gien me a brave thick bit o steak"*, not heard often I'll grant you). Where we part company with standard English is the use of thick as a indication of a person's character.

If an Ulster Scot describes an individual as being *"thick"*, it is not a measurement of their IQ or there ability to do (*tae dae*) differential calculus in their head (*heid*). Rather it is an indication that the person being described is a stubborn individual, not easily given to compromise or a poor prospect in the field of negotiation. ("*Thon yin, he's as thick as champ*"; *"champ"*, as *the maist o ye wull dootless be awar*, having *naethin tae dae* **wae** the shortened address to a successful boxer but rather being a dish of *prootas an scallions (*spring onions*) wae a guid drap o butter ower the tap an a washed doon wae a jug o coul buttermilk* (this last being optional an **whiles knowed** as *"soordook"*). *"Champ"* is *"brave pakkin"*, a dense and nourishing dish with a habit *"o stickin tae yer ribs"*. *"Thick"* here also means difficult and a person so described might be highly intelligent but prone to mood swings and therefore needing careful handling and the application of diplomatic skills.

"***Thick***" is often used as a cognate for "***thran***", an adjective used to indicate an awkward individual or job but also meaning twisted, its origin being from "***thra***" meaning to be awkward and intractable or given to arguing and hair splitting.

To suggest that "***Him an him's very thick***" is not to cast aspersions on the intellectual abilities of the gentlemen under discussion but means instead that the lads in question are friendly. The expression carries an implication that this friendship might not be a healthy one and this may be an indication that there is a link to the expression "***as thick as thieves***".

If a boady was said "***tae tak it thick***" this would not be a signifier of a preference in milk shakes but would instead carry the meaning that the person in question had taken offence ("***I argied aboot the money an he tuk it thick***" and such a person, having "***taen it thick***" might then "***tak thick***" meaning having taken offence, they might then turn stubborn and nasty.

The BBC television series, "**The Thick of It**", means the same in Ulster Scots as in standard English, that is "**the middle of it**" but perhaps it could also be rendered as "***up tae yer oxters in it***", in other words, "**sunk in something to the depth your armpits**" although this may not catch fully the intended irony in the title of Armando Iannucci's creation which I am certain intends to hint at the "stupid" sense of "thick".

An Ulster Scots Memory

Society was ordered differently back in the 1950s and 60s when I was a wean. Yes there was poverty, yes there was need, but people shared that state and shared so much else besides. No nursing homes, no elderly persons homes, no homes for the mentally infirm. Older people were managed in the community, with the label "doting" attached. This indicated a tendency to start conversations from the middle, a predilection for argument and raised voice when alone and an ability to fall asleep at unexpected times, on occasion in mid sentence.

"Dote" was also a term of affection applied to a particularly loved wean, often rendered as "a wee dote" and couples were said to "dote " on each other, although this state of bliss was usually confined to the early days of the marriage, and not a huge number of days either. If someone were confused or forgetful or mistaken in a big way, they might be berated by being said to be "doting", a state that could be achieved after a surprisingly short period of marriage.

The "non-doting" elderly, who had passed beyond self-management, tended to be domiciled within a wider family circle on a rotational basis, oft times your own, the odd time someone close. One such was an elderly uncle of mine, we'll call him Uncle Pat. Of course, in a sense it goes without saying that he was not my uncle. He was in fact my great uncle, being my Granny's brother and he had reached his autumn years without a roof for his head. He was an occasional but regular visitor and looking back now, I can see clearly that there was a cycle to these visitations. I didn't notice it then. Uncle Pat enjoyed a lifestyle which seemed to me then (and sometimes even now) to represent the apotheosis of good living. He rose late, never before half ten, rarely after half eleven, and partook of a hearty breakfast; porridge, boiled egg and toast alternating with a fry, all accompanied with hot sweet tea. Here, Pat enjoyed yet another of his many privileges, all denied to youth; he liked his tea hot so in order to cool it sufficiently for his mouth, he poured his tea into his saucer and blew on it. He then supped the by now slightly cooled infusion directly from the saucer and damn the hair did he care how much noise he made during this process. It was a visual and aural taunt; had we attempted any of these actions a swift clash on the lug would have ensued. The great tay ritual, I have always assumed it to be distantly related to the Japanese version, was followed unfailingly by the first pipe of the day, the smell of War Horse as redolent of lost times as any French madeleine.

Despite the late hour of breakfast, his enthusiasm for the mid-day meal (I recollect it being called it dinner then but nowadays most of us know it as lunch) was utterly undimmed and he passed himself more than adequately at the kitchen table. And it was at the table that Pat indulged in another of his personal dispensations from normal etiquette; he never removed his cap, a flat cap with a peak, called on occasion a duncher.

Not even when he shaved, or was shaved, did the cap come off. I never saw him in the tin bath so it may have stayed on even there; I certainly like to think so. I suppose the barber's was different.

Postprandial activity consisted of a return to the fireside from which he surveyed life and critiqued the world, between puffs on his briar pipe, the steuch of which permeated the entire house, not as big a task as that phrase implies. It was here that he exercised yet another privilege far beyond our wildest dreams. He spat regularly into the fire, an action that had we, the weans, attempted it would have resulted in our severe and immediate chastisement, probably with another clash on the lug. My Aunt Annie assures me that on occasion his expectorations would catch fire with a whoosh due to the alcoholic content.

He had been a shepherd all his days in the hills above Armoy and had a seemingly inexhaustible supply of horror stories, mostly but not always about late night confrontations with otherworldly creatures, usually ending in death, disfigurement or hair trauma (discolouration or loss). The dead, it seemed, rested uneasily in Armoy Glen and apparently held a grudge agin the hirsute.

There was almost always a smell of burning somewhere (in the stories, I mean) and the odd whiff of sulphur, denoting the presence of the Evil One. Probably related to his work with sheep, although I never made the connection at the time, was his wide range of whistling skills, and whether using only his lips or finger (or indeed fingers assisted), he could have been a session whistler for any God's amount of disco records had he but been born fifty years later and relocated to New York.

Like all old stagers, he appreciated an audience, even if it only consisted of credulous weans, wide-eyed and slack-jawed, all united in our determination never to venture to that far corner of the globe that was Armoy Glen, particularly after dark. I suppose I've never lost that fear of Armoy.
Or shepherding.
Or farmwork in general for that matter.
Or, indeed, work.

He was a kindly man and a good-natured man who was both patient with and indulgent to unbearded youth.

Uncle Pat also imparted wisdom about more domestic subjects such as the management of a peat fire. The door of the black lead range was almost always open and the peats that fuelled it lay stacked brave and handy.
Pat explained that the way to extract maximum energy from the peat, though he may not have employed exactly that phraseology, was to leave the fire totally undisturbed rather than poking it, as was done with the crown of slack left from the previous night.

Given that Uncle Pat's diet was centred on fried food, full cream milk, full fat butter, eggs and as much red meat as could be afforded. I suppose it was to be expected, indeed, inevitable that there would be consequences for his health. His affection for tobacco and the craiter didn't help.

And indeed so it proved and Pat was snatched from us in an untimely fashion at the tender age of ninety-six. And he passed on without ever passing into his dotage.

Sam Mary Anne

Of coorse there definitely wus mair characters aboot years ago; there wus a lock less tak aboot TV and a lock mair interest in the real world an the folk that leeved in it. Yin weel knowed an weel laiked boady was a man naw noted for his sartorial elegance who traded under the name of Hashter Gemmlc. Hashter combined the troosers fray yin suit way the jacket o anither an apparently very little debate aboot style o shirt, tie or socks, if they wur available.

If a boady happened to appear in a dishevelled state, they wur aye compared tae Hashter Gemmle.

Noo A hay tay confess I never met Hashter but I did see him mair nor yince. Anither character hails frae an earlier time, bak tae the days o me Fether an Mother, an I niver seen him but he was ca'ed Sam Mary Anne. Sam Mary Anne hailed frae somewhere between Bellycastle an Armoy. He, an for the purposes o oor yarn the day we'll call him a he, he discovered at an early age that he was a lock mair comfortable dressed up in weemen's claes naw men's attire. An bein a big boady wi airms on him laik legs and fists laik hams, when he tuk it intay his heed tay slip oan a skirt an a matchin handbag, naeb'dy toul him there wus onythin wrang wae daein it. An nether there wus.

This boady, Sam Mary Anne, went tay his work kitted oot as a female and went tae dances in the Quay Road Hall in Bellycastle an naeb'dy bothered him. Well, A say naeb'dy bothered him; me Da maintains he wus danced aff his feet by the men o the Glens, young an oul, an if a han strayed onywhere sooth o the equator, Sam Mary Anne wusnay lang minin him o his manners. He was a real stickler fur etiquette. He rid tay the dances an a roon the country on a women's bike an naeb'dy passed ony remarks, naw within his hearin ony road.

The main thing aboot this hale shemozzle wus that folk understood difference in them days, people respected individuality an didnae feel the need tay persecute them that stood oot frae the herd. Folk tholed ither yins way o gan becas it wus the mannerly thing tay dae.
An people didnae judge ye jist bay the claes
ye wur wearin.

I know naethin o Sam Mary
Anne's ither activities, proclivities
or lifestyle choices an A'll tell yes
aal noo, A dinnae care. Well
maybe A'm a bit curious but
in a scientific wie, naethin
prurient. There's lessons
could be learned for the
day aboot toleration,
respect an difference.

A'm sure an certain
the yin thing Sam
Mary Anne would laik
aboot the day is ether the
Manolo Blahniks or the
Jimmy Choo's.

The Beverly Hillbillies

In the multi channel digital age that is oor ain brave new worl the day, it's naw aisy tay convey the effect that a single half 'oor television programme cud hae on the hale country. Fer that metter, the notion o TV takin ower frae radio wus a newance. Since there wur jist the two television stations, three if you counted RTE, they modern TV stations could only dream of this level of impact.

A mean ye definitely wur getting the same waal tay waal coverage the same as say "Big Brother" or "A'm A Naeb'dy, Resurrect may Career" or whatever it's ca'ed. But the laugh track did whiles seem a bit inappropriate. The things that the Americans seemed tae fin funny didnae seem jist as funny tae me.

The femly was decidedly non nuclear. Jed's a widower wae yin daughter frae the union, the beautiful and voluptuous Ellie Mae, a girl who was allus interested in fun.

Granny, even though she was Jed's mither in la, leeved at hame wae the rest o thim, naethin odd or funny there, monies a granny leeved at hame wae their relatives in oor country. Plus Grannie was a self proclaimed M.D. (a mountain doctor) with a knowledge and faith in poultices and unorthodox medicine; nooadays, Prince Charles would be spakin up for her; that hale "wise woman" thing definitely chimed wae us who were aye getting bread poultices fer ivry ill. Granny also cooked with a griddle ower an open fire and made her ain breed An made her ain whiskey tae. These wus baith activities weel knowed all aboot oor country. Jethro Bodine was Jed's nephew thrown on tae the hospitality o the Clampetts by fate. They wernae used tae indoor plumbin, it was a newance tae them an us baith. Jed was in the wae o shootin for the pot, naethin strange up in oor pairt o the worl. The dourbell flummoxed them an it was a new sound tae us tae. Thon was a fancy toon thing. At hame whiles there was a knock but the maist o yins jist come on in. An they used tae come in in their droves on the nights the "Beverly Hillbillies" was on An noo they tell me there's an Ulster Scots connection.

Accordin tae the Ulster Scots Agency's website, the term "Billie Boys" haes naethin tae dae wae Oor Wullie o Orange De ye naw know that the term **"billie boys"** comes frae the Scots word "billie" meaning a freen or a brother. So the "billie boys" historically refers to a group of friends, a fraternity or a brotherhood. An of coorse if there was a wheen o yins leevin in the hills, laik the Ozarks or the Appalachians, then it wud be only but natural tae ca the "billies frae the hills" or for that metter, "hill-billies". Ye can see hoo thon story cud get picked up wrang an something made o it that isnae there.

Ony road, the Clampetts an Bodeanes and Moses's (because Granny was Daisy Mae Moses) they wur a hospitable lock o folk an they laiked bluegrass music played wi banjos an so did we. So the theme music was a hit naw only for the music but the words as weel.

Able Was I Ere I Saw Elba

While on the theme of words where our local usage shares **a wheen o** the meanings in Standard English but **naw al**, a good example would be "**able**". Now, of course, there is the shared meaning of the common application in Standard English as a gauge of capability, of having the requisite physical strength, mental power, money, skill, time or opportunity to do or achieve something. There is also the shared meaning in the sense of being clever or good at what you do.

However, there is a divergence of meaning from Standard English, the Ulster Scots meaning of "**able** " is not usually complimentary. It means cunning, crafty, shrewd (in the business sense) and quick witted. "**A wile able boady**" would be someone with whom it would not normally be advisable to trade or treat. Such an individual was deemed to possess the ability to "**tak an eye oot o yer heid an tell ye ye wur betther lukkin wae yin**". This meaning of "**able**" as full of guile was an attribute occasionally attaching to city dwellers or for that matter, town dwellers but not exclusively so, there were a brave wheen o able yins throughout the country, rural and urban.

Another description of an "**able**" person would be the Scots word "**sleekit**" meaning devious, treacherous or sly ("**A dinnae care what ye say there a wile sleekit thing aboot him an A dinnae laik it yin bit**").

Of course, Burns famously used the term but it was more in the sense of smooth

> **(Wee, sleekit, cow'rin', tim'rous beastie,**
> **O what a panic's in thy breastie!**
> **Thou need na start awa sae hasty,**
> **Wi' bickerin' brattle!**
> **I wad be laith to rin an' chase thee**
> **Wi' murd'rin' pattle!)**

A man, or for that matter, a woman who was "**able for**" an opponent, whether in a physical contest, a mental joust or a verbal clash was usually adjudged to be someone who was more than (**mair nor**) a match for their protagonist. Being "**able wae the tongue**" meant the ability "**tae dish oot a tonguing**", the modern equivalent, perhaps, being a tongue lashing.

There is also the sense of "**ability**" as physical strength or stamina, usually noted in the absence ("**It disnae metter what A dae, A hae nae ability at a**").

The antithesis of "**able**" is "**saft**", ("**He's that saft, a wean cud buy an sell him**"). People would be encouraged to adopt a more realistic approach to a situation ("**Dinnae be so saft**") or an individual could be assessed as being slightly more worldly than might appear at first glance ("**He's naw as saft as he luks**"). And if a man or woman (or for that matter, a child) were deemed to be not in the least bit "**saft**", the judgement might be handed down that the "**the saftest thing aboot him (or her) is his (or her) teeth**". Such a person would be adjudged to be the very embodiment of "**able**".

The Yin an Oany

There were oany yin thing tae be writ aboot in this piece and that's what oany sensible bein would hae oan their mine at the minute.

"Oany" is the Ulster Scots rendition of two words from Standard English, **nether o thim related till the ither,** "*only* "and "*any*". Admittedly, the former use, for "*only*", is less common and the majority of use is for "*any*".

Of course its use as a prefix mirrors that of Standard English, as in **"onyboady"**, meaning anybody or in a wider sense, a reasonable man, or indeed, a principled or decent man. Or indeed woman. (" **If he was oanybody at al, he wud gae it bak an say naethin mair aboot it**"). '*Anyplace*' is rendered as **"oanyplace"** ("**A wushed it'd been oanyplace only ootside oor hoose (or oooris)** ") and '*anyway*' comes oot as **"oanyroad"** (" **Ah'm gan tae gower an see her oanyroad**"), although "**oanyroad**" can also be used to convey '*in any way whatsoever*' (" **Luck see, Ah'm naw interested, oany road**").

If you were possessed of a significant quantity of "**oanythin**", a surplus, a cornucopia, an abundance, one might be said to " **hae oany God's amount o**" the material in question.

There is also a meaning, "**for oany sake**", which would equate to *'for goodness sake* ', usually in the form of an entreaty or an appeal ("**For oany sake, daenae be sayin oanythin aboot it tae ether o them**"). There is a meaning of oany which conveys the sense of "*to any extent* ", ("**Is haes health improved oany?**").

A further interpretation of "**laik oanythin**" can be the sense of "*a presentable state* " or "*fit for purpose*" ("**If it's laik oanythin at a, it'll hae tae dae** ").

I am indebted to Mr. Jim Nesbitt of Coleraine, a retired schoolmaster with wide teaching experience throughout North Antrim for the following story. I recently met Jim (**an a lock o ither yins forby**) at the monthly **getherin o** the Coleraine Historical Society **an gye hospitable they al wur tae**. Jim **toul** me he overheard the following exchange between two pupils in a County Antrim school playground, one possessed of a packet of sweets, one not. (And apologies if I **hae got any o they pairts wrang**). "**Gie us yin**" quoth our hungry schoolboy. Replied his pal, through a **moothfu' o** sweets,

"**A wud if A cud but A haenae yin tae gie ye so A cannae gie ye ony**".

Maister Nesbitt **didnae** tell me how **lang** ago the exchange **tuk** place but I'm guessing it was a day or two bak. Isn't it funny how things stick in **yer mine**.

Howl Yer Horses

Howl oan a minit till I gether me thouchts. "Howl" in Ulster Scots has no relationship with the noise escaping from a discombobulated, dismayed, disquieted, distressed or disturbed **doag** or **houn**. That, as *any fule kno*, is a **"gowl"**, perhaps best known in the phrase " **a baigle's gowl**" as an indication of distance, most commonly as an indication of the distance from the intended answer, target or destination ("**He wasnae inside (or within) a baigle's gowl o it**" or indeed, "**baigles' gowls o it**"). "**Howl**" equates in the majority of instances to the Standard English "hold". A "**howldin**" would be a reference to a holding or parcel or farm of land.

Local readers will be familiar with the term "**howl yer wheesht**" meaning keep quiet or keep your counsel. Sometimes rendered as "**howl yer tongue**" or in moments of discombobulation, this might be shortened (to match one's temper) to "**shut yer gob**", conveying almost the same meaning but with additional emotional impact. "**Howl yer wheesht**" can also be shortened to "**Wheesht!**", an example of the use of the Ulster Scots vocative case with onomatopoeic overtones (or possibly undertones). A bargain was commonly sealed, in more trusting times, by two men, and it was usually men, "**howlin oot their han**", often after spitting on the palm and shaking. "**Howlin yer han**" was to stay your actions, to keep your power dry for the meantime, to hold back, to proceed with some caution, possibly as a preamble to the application "**o the bak o yer han**", either a physical rebuff or a metaphoric one ("**If ye're gan tae tak thick, the bak o me han tae ye**") or indeed, "**takkin the han**", making fun of or making sport with (modern equivalent perhaps "You're having a laugh!").

"**Howl up**" could be either an instruction to a recalcitrant horse to keep its head up or possibly a request to a fleet footed friend to proceed at a more decorous pace. Another usage of "howl up" is in relation to the weather; will the good (or bad) weather continue ("**Will it (*rain, hail or shine*) howl up?**").

"**Howl**" also has a use in relation to gambling, real or conversational. A speculative comment about a likely event or outcome might be accompanied by the statement "**A'll howl ye for tuppence**". ("**A'll howl ye for tuppence it was her that done it**" "**A'll howl ye for tuppence there'll be naeb'dy there only himsel**"). Although larger amounts might be metaphorically wagered, the small amount was usually an indication of likelihood and thus a disincentive to hazard even such a derisory sum. By the way, not quite such a derisory an amount when I was a **weechil**.

Another phrase incorporating the word "**howl**" to mean "hold" is "**howl fit tae**" meaning to continue or sustain or keep up with ("**A'll naw can howl fit tae the rippin' an tearin' o him much langer.**"). Those of a diplomatic bent, blessed with the ability to maintain a dignified silence when confronted with provocation, could be said to be have the ability "**tae howl in**". There is also the sense of being watertight or airtight.

On a less scientific note, or at least an unproven theory, when the crescent moon is tilted, it is said to be "**howlin in**" and the weather would be expected to be fair. When the moon is upright, it is referred to as "**rinnin oot**" and a consequent decline in meteorological conditions, usually leading to rain, might be expected.

Getting Ouler

I think it was Wullie Shakespeare who identified seven ages of man. The Ulsterman is a bit **mair** generous **wae** the numbers and there are several ages of man, and indeed, woman, identified in Ulster Scots.

Afore ye were **boarn**, **yer Ma** (or your Mother) might be said **tae** be in the **femly wie** or indeed, **"wae a wain"**. Upon entering the Vale of Tears, the happy couple, if couple there were, might be said "**tae hae hed their first ba**" or indeed "**their twelfth ba**". Families were bigger a while **bak**, but a twelfth **yin's naw sae laikly noo**.

After a short interval, a **ba** can be transmogrified **intae** a "**bairn**" but this would tend to be an affected reference, the much more common usage would be "**wain**" (or occasionally "**wean**") which is itself a cognate for "**bairn**" but most likely derived from "**wee yin**". A young family ("**femly**") would be "**bits o wains**" ("**It's gye hard work for them wae naethin but bits o wains aboot them**"). There is also a derogatory use of "**wains**" to describe help or assistance rendered inadequate due to relative youth ("**We would a needed a wheen o men tae dae thon job but a we got was bits o wains**").

Up to this point, the **maist** of the references I have alluded to, do not differentiate on grounds of gender. "**Weetchil**" is a term for a young person, more often applied to boys rather than girls.

After a period of time (I was going to hazard that at one time the transition point was the transfer from short trousers to long but I fear that may no longer be applicable), a "**weetchil**" ("**wee child**") becomes a "**weefla**", obviously a contraction of '**wee fella**'. This is, of course, highly gender specific i.e. male. The female equivalent might be identified as a "**wee hizzy**".

After another time period, the "**hobbledhoy**" appears, ("**He's a hobbledehoy, nether a man nor a boy**"), again clearly male with a female version perhaps being "**cutty**" although "**cutty**" as a term of identity has a longer shelf life than "**hobbledhoy**" and might be used in reference to an **ouler yin**..

I well remember the Reverend Ian Paisley advising Mrs Thatcher (for younger readers, she was a politician from a long time ago, and not young when he said it), and I paraphrase slightly, that "She may think she's an Iron Lady but over here she's just a Tin Cutty".

It **wasnae jist** the Ulster Scots speakers that knew exactly what he meant.

A Drap O the Craiter

Every time I see Mrs. Doyle in the wonderful "**Father Ted**" insisting on providing some hapless individual (not always a cleric) with a cup of tea, regardless of whether it was wanted or needed, I am transported back to my youth and the tea ritual, every bit as formal as the Japanese Tea Ceremony, associated with the arrival of a visitor. The proffered "**drap o tay**" was inevitably too much bother for so humble a visitor and the Mrs. Doyle routine was replicated almost exactly as Arthur Mathews and Graham Linehan (the creators of "**Father Ted**") have suggested.

Eventually, after much convoluted negotiation, a compromise was reached, usually a "**drap in yer hand**", usually indicating a cup (full of tea) along with a saucer and the phrase is, I think, meant to *indicate that there was no necessity to sit down at a table.* In days gone by, the **tay** was put into the saucer to cool and, "**boysadears**", did I think that was cool (in the modern sense of the word). My mother was less enthused of this practice but wouldn't utter a word to a visitor. Her tongue was less restrained on us weans.

The question of accompaniment to "**yer tay**", perhaps in the shape of a "wee bun" (home made or shop bought) or a Rich Tea, occupied a whole separate argument.

"**Drap**" in Standard English equates to "**drop**" but as with other words, it has additional Ulster Scots resonances. A "**drap o' tay**" oft times not only involved the golden liquid from the Orient but a light snack or collation "**forby**".

"**A bad drap**" indicates the possession of an evil side to your character ("**There a powerfu' bad drap in him an it's naw aff the bak dorr he taks it**"; in other words, "There's a vicious side to him and he gets it from his home rather than any outside influences"). "**Drop off**" in Standard English usually means to slip into the Land of Nod but in Ulster Scots, "**drap aff**" also means to die, as does "**cowp**" or "**cope**", a slang variation on the general meaning of spill, tip up or overturn.

If "**ye wur drappin aff yer feet**", you were close to exhaustion. To "**drap prootas**" was to plant them by hand but to be "**fond o a wee drap**" usually indicated a preference for a liquid something a little stronger than Orange Pekoe, usually alcoholic and usually in quantities greater than the term "**drap**" might be thought to indicate.

Twa Het and Yin Ra

In light of the good weather, apparently all due to global warming and excess carbon emissions, I thought I'd reflect on the Ulster Scots treatment of temperature.

"**Het**" is, of course, the Ulster Scots rendition of hot and might be applied to the weather ("**It was gye het yesterday**" meaning "**The weather was particularly clement yesterday**") but also applicable in a number of other instances.

A spoilt or unruly or cheeky child who might benefit from the application of some minor corporal punishment could be said "**to need his erse weel het**" meaning "**He could do with a smack to the hindquarters**". Obviously such physical chastisement for your little darlings is frowned upon but once upon a time 'twas commonplace.

Such retribution as might be visited on the offspring (or whoever) legally could be delivered with great severity or "**het an reekin**" as the Ulster Scots hae it, though to be fair, this referred to verbal redress rather than physical. So if "**het an reekin**" were to indicate that no punches were pulled, these would be metaphorical punches rather than tremendous haymakers or, in Ulster Scots "**a sevendible**". Another use of "**het**" is in the phrase "het stitch" meaning straight away, without hesitation or in a full blown manner ("**Yin thing led tae anither an afore ye could blink, they wur at it het stitch**"). An exceptionally fine day was "**a bleezer**" not to be confused with the attire of a rugby (or any other sport's) alick-a-doos, the blazer.

The antithesis of "**het**" is "**cowl**" meaning cold. Another variant on "**cowl**" is "**starvin**" or "**stairvin**". While I am familiar with its use (shared with standard English) in relation to hunger ("**I was starving wae hunger**"), the more common usage of "**starvin**" relates to low temperature ("**He sut us doon in thon front room wae nae heat; it would 'a starved ye**"). An individual lacking in charity, compassion or the milk of human kindness might be referred to as a "**coul Christian**" or a "**cowl cretter**" and one so lacking in blood as to be particularly conscious of low temperatures was reckoned to be "**cowl rife**". One cure I heard proffered for this condition was the consumption of a duck egg for breakfast, a prescription which allegedly thickened the blood though I can't comment on its efficacy.

Another cure for the "**cowl**" was the consumption of strong waters or spirits ("**the craiter**"). James Fenton tells me a tale of whiskey and a Bellamoney pub. He observed three gentlemen entering Kelly's in Bellamoney (a pub long since gone). Approaching the bar, the first man spoke to the proprietor; "**Twa het an yin ra**" quoth he. Without a blink, the landlord proceeded to prepare our three topers two hot whiskeys and one without any artificial additives, flavourings or colouring. Jim never mentioned whether it was "**het**" or "**cowl**" **thon** day but in my mind, "**it wud a starved ye**"

Yin Nought Yin

If Ulster Scots were to be boiled down to a single word, one individual standard bearer for the entire tongue, there would of course be many candidates, possibly even arguments as to the validity of such a process. Nevertheless, I would suggest that a credible contender might be the word "**yin**" meaning, to the uninitiated, "one".

First of all, let's not confuse this latter with the homonym, "**wun**", equating to the Standard English "wind" or "breath", prevalent in such phrases as " **a wun that wud clean coarn**" ("a breeze with a significant wind chill factor") or "**A haenae the wun tae dae a this rinnin**" ("I'm out of breath after running about") or indeed, "**Keep yer wun tae cool yer parridge**" ("Don't waste your breath giving advice"). The Ulster Scots also suffered grievously with "**wun**" which could cause "**rifts**" or even more embarrassing eructations (burps). Or, indeed, other leakages of intestinal gas.

Apart from cardinal usage ("**yin single thing**"), its presence is noteworthy in a number of expressions; "**A'll tell ye yin thing an that's naw two**" ("Allow me to emphasise or clarify") might be heard from a strong minded and opinionated person. "**A the yin thing** " or "**A yin**" indicates homogeneity in apparently differing propositions. If a person undertook to "**gie ye yin**" as a reward for an ill turn, it usually meant the use of physical force. If him and her were "**the yin age** ", they (supposedly) had coincident years since birth. Although even Ulster Scots were sometimes a little economical with the *actualité* regarding age. Among the most famous (or infamous) uses of "yin" was as a stick to beat County Antrim Orangemen. Legend has it that the Orange Lodge in Cullybackey was designated LOL 101 (Loyal Orange Lodge One Hundred and One) rendered by Belfast (half) wits as **Yin Not Yin** (as opposed to **Yin Nought Yin**). Following consultations with an esteemed Orange historian, I am assured that LOL 101 was located in Portadown rather than Cullybackey.

So much for legends.

Put Ye in Mine O' Somethin'

"**Mine**" in Ulster Scots is akin to the Standard English "**mind**" but it gets used in a much wider variety of guises than its English equivalent while still sharing a number of uses.

"**The langest thing A mine**" would be a person's earliest memory and this meaning of remembering has a number of instances in the hamely tongue. "**A can mine whun there wuz naethin oany fiels a roon here**" recalls an earlier and more agricultural version of the fast disappearing green belt. "**Did ye mine tae bring it wae ye?**" is a test most of our memories occasionally fail. This remembering can also apply to a situation where a greeting is being sent ("**Mine me tae yer Mother**") There is the use of "mine" meaning observation or regard ("**Wud ye mine the cut o yer man**" indicates that "*That chap's sartorial choices [or unsteady gait or facial expressions] are well worth your immediate and undivided attention*").

There is also the use of "mine" as "remind" ("**He mines me o yer Da**" "*He has an uncanny resemblance to your father*" "**He mines me o' a wee boady A used tae work wae**" or "**Mine me tae tak thon thing wae me the morra**" " *Try and jog my failing memory into recollecting the necessity of bringing that article with me on the morrow*").

"**Mine**" can be used to indicate the phrase "*strike one as*" as in "**He mines me on a boy worth keepin yer eye on**" "*That individual strikes me as being not as trustworthy as one would wish in an ideal world*".

And of course, as a request to move ("**Mine oot o me wie**") or a (friendly) warning to be careful ("**Mine yersel noo**").

It's my sincere hope that reading this has taken your mind off a worry or perhaps raised your spirits somewhat. If it has done that, it might be said "**tae hae lifted yer mine**".

Thon Ulster Scots Book

Tak a Han Ooty

A thoucht A'd try me han at "**han**". "**Han**" in Ulster Scots equates largely to the Standard English "**hand**" but as with so many other Ulster Scots words, it gets **streetched tae fit a big lock o uses** (*stretched in a wide variety of ways*).

Assessments of the quality of an individual's abilities to discharge or perform certain duties might vary from the sublime ("**He's a dab han wae the paintbrush**" [*He can paint a bit*] or the sarcastic "**He's dab han at daein naethin an gettin weel pied for it**", a comment on an overpaid slacker) to the incompetent or the unskilled ("**He's a bad han at onythin tae dae wae beasts**", a person with no natural aptitude for the animal kingdom, agricultural, domestic or otherwise). A "**sad han**" or a "**sore han**" indicates a poorly executed task; ("**Thon builder made a sad han o thon porch**", a comment that might be used by an architectural critic about a small bit of building work). Should general skill levels, in whatever field of endeavour, be of a particularly low standard, an individual may be identified as "**hanless**": indeed anyone lacking in manual dexterity can be thus described, as could anyone awkward or clumsy in whatever limb. Such a person may be said to "**hae hans for naethin**".

In the work environment, this sort of worker would rarely be allowed to remain in employment long enough to be characterised as an "**oul han**" (*an experienced artisan*), an epithet also applicable to old friends and neighbours (**nighbours** or **neibors**, **drouthy** or otherwise). A piece of work or work in general could be described as a "**han's turn**" ("**She niver daes a hans turn roon the hoose frae she rises til she lies doon**", a remark aimed at a slattern).

A favourable circumstance would "**lie tae yer han**", allowing a person to "**tak the thing in han**" (*take something on*) on a "**handy**" (*felicitous or propitious*) basis.

Any piece of mischief, any frolic or indeed, waggishness of any stripe carried out on anybody was a case of "**takkin the han ooty a boady**".

CALENDAR POEM

January

Whun there's mair rid nebs nor midges
An ye need yer wellin'ton boots,
The snow is lyin roon in wreaths
An the snowdraps ir jist keekin oot.

February

Whun young yins thouchts turn tae coortin
It's nae tim fur fear o the cowl;
The yows is ready fur lammin
An the hird haes nae time tae scowl.

March

We wunner if Paddy micht help us
Heel ower the dry side o the stane;
They're cloddin the britchin on horses
For there's plooin that haes tae be daen.

April

Mair aften than no there's a brave plump o rain,
It's sae guid fur the gairden an fiel;
The green o the hedge an the floors al aroon -
Och daesn't the country luk weel!

May

The ha's a' in bloom, the epple tree tae,
An the cherry tree's castin its floors;
Way a lassie ye laik in a place that ye laik
A minute can streetch in tae oors.

June

Simmertim's here an school's near ower,
There's peats tae be cut in the moss;
There's fittin an sweetin an naethin for pie -
Sich labour wud mak a saint cross!

July

Them yins that mairches awa tae the fiel
Can work up a druth thru the day;
Whur ither yins gan a bit farder awa
Ir aiblins a bit druthy tae.

August

Thon peats that ye cut in May or in June
Is dry enugh noo for the stak,
An gin that the rodden's no slunky or wat
The folk'll be cairtin them bak.

September

The simmer is ower, the holiday by,
The weans hae a gye heavy hert,
For it's bak tae school way pencil an piece
An a bag big enugh for a cairt.

October

Scobin at epples an getherin prootas
Yer fingers a' blue wi the cowl,
Yer bak doobled ower wi wile stoons o pain -
Jist sixpence a bag, deed sowl!

November

Misty an reekie an nae time til dark
But gled o the fire an the heat;
Feared o the wraiths when ye hae tae goot
Tae the shade for an ermful o peat.

December

Santy's the boady tae bring yez yer toys
We see the weans wile joy again,
Weechils an cutties an hobbledehoys
Micht aiblins mine thon ither Wean.

A Dig in the Bake

To an untrained observer, there appears to be a renaissance in the art of baking; witness the irresistible (no doubt yeast inspired) rise of the baking television programme. However, not all meanings of bake relate to the use of a dry heated oven.

I have had a couple of inquiries about "bake"; one wondered if it was the word for 'book' (naw is the answer, that's "buik", by the way) and the other wanted to know the origin in general (I'm old but not that old).
The origin is, to my mind, an area for speculation but we can look at the use and meaning to the Ulster Scots.

"Bake" is shorthand for mouth and its use is usually indicative of an insulting and aggressive demeanour.

A noisy outburst or the casting of aspersions on the reputation of an individual or organisation might result in an exhortation to "Shut yer bake!" ("Let's keep the volume at manageable levels" or "Kindly withdraw that gratuitous slur").

Failure to comply with the suggested course of action could have implications of a physical nature and may result in the application of a "slap in the bake" or a "dig in the bake" (physical chastisement aimed primarily at the mouth utilising either an open hand or a closed fist). A hearty eater might be described as "stuffing his or her bake" when engaged at the table in an enthusiastic and uninhibited manner. Whether the bill of fare on offer is boiled, fried, roasted or baked is rarely of interest to an Ulster Scot "stuffin their bake".

The origin is, I think, "beak" (as in a bird's beak) but if you have any other ideas about this, dinnae keep them tae yersel an dinnae keep yer bake shut. In fact, open yer bake.

Can't be Bate

"Bate" in English means hold back, restrain, lessen or diminish. In Ulster Scots it's a different story a thegither.

In Ulster Scots, if you're bate, you could have lost a game or contest (A'm bate; I am defeated) (She bate me fair and square; she used all her feminine wiles to bamboozle me and eventually I was cheated of my rightful victory), you could have been on the receiving end of a damned good thrashing ("He got a terrible batin the ither evenin"; he was takkin when he should have been listenin an some dacent boady explained the difference).

If an enterprise or endeavour is deemed beyond redemption, it can be referred to as a "baten docket", a reference to losing betting slips provided at the local turf accountant's.

After a hard day's work (younger readers should ask an appropriate adult what this is), it is conceivable that an individual might be heard to remark "A'm bate" meaning "I am tired from my exertions and may require some down-time to recover".

The "bate o" something or other usually indicates a superior, larger or more impressive specimen or event ("A niver seen the bate o thon boys fightin"; "A niver seen the bate o thon match the ither evenin"). And if an item or event is to one's satisfaction or delight, it usually "cudnae be bate" or even "ye cudnae bate it wae a big stick".

There is a particular use of "bater" or "baters" which is, as far as I am aware, peculiar to the Ballymoney area, meaning heels or feet, so to "tak tae yer baters" means to run as fast as you can, to take to your heels, to sprint away.

Am gan tae tak tae me baters noo.

A Cheeky Blert

Let's settle something straight away, the spelling. Some folk favour "blirt"; I don't. And there's no connection to "blurt", in Standard English, an abrupt utterance, an ejaculation, to divulge inadvertently.

"Blert" is, unusually for Ulster Scots (!), a term of abuse but differs in the main from the general terms of abuse since it doesn't refer to any innate lack of ability, application or good appearance but is rather a criticism of an individual's mean spiritedness or nasty nature.

Since it takes a range of qualifiers and modifiers (an ignorant blert; less well-mannered than might be hoped for: a dirty blert; not an honourable person), there are a range of strengths applicable; "a cheeky blert" or "ye big blert" might be used in a light hearted sense among friends. It's less likely that a humourous interpretation would be put on a "dirty blert", though to some extent it depends on the context.

And if you hear someone comment about "that blert of a referee", you can safely assume there's little carefree or happy in the remark.

By and large, the use of "blert" betokens a nasty, offensive and objectionable person. Apart from the heartlands of Ulster Scots where it is heard the odd time (there being so few nasty, offensive and objectionable Ulster Scots people), it is rarely heard in wider society nowadays whereas it was in common usage when I was a wean.

Obviously there may be a lot less useless blerts in the country.
I can't say I've noticed.

Blatter Away

Naw, naething tae dae with FIFA and Sepp of that ilk (a man who thought WW2 should have been resolved with a handshake), "blatter" means to strike, to hit; it is frequently but not exclusively used in the context of physical combat (He hut him a quare blatter and there wasnae anither word ooty 'im) (He blattered him that hard he was oot coul).

"Blatter" can be used in relation to drumming (He hut thon bass drum a blatter). He was blatterin away at thon snare drum that hard it wud a deefened ye)

Can also mean a loud sound associated with a blow or a strike (There was a blatter at the wunda that scarred the wuts oot a me)) and can be interchanged with brattle in relation to thunder (a brattle or blatter o thunder).

"Clatter"

In English, it can mean a noise ("making a clatter") or indeed a deliberate collision or strike, perhaps a football tackle ("He clattered into him") but in Ulster Scots it means a number ("I went there thinkin I knew naebdy but I knew a clatter o' them" "We wur close tae closin when a clatter o young yins landed in") but exactly what number is a matter of speculation, though context is important.

In my mind, it's quite a few ("a brave wheen"), probably north of six or seven but as well as meaning a specific number, it can also used to indicate an unexpectedness of the numbers, more than expected ("They toul me there wur only supposed tae be yin or two but a clatter o them come").

Mak ye Boak

Some Ulster Scots words are so deeply ensconced in our everyday speech that many people don't recognise them as Ulster Scots, "boak" being a good case in point.

"Boak" basically means to vomit but it has as many uses in a metaphorical sense as it has in relation to physical well-being, or the lack thereof. A useful term, it can be a verb ("When he starts thon oul bummin an blowin, it would mak ye boak"; his constant self-promotion would turn your stomach) or a noun ("He's a boak"; he's a person whose behaviour engenders in me an irresistible urge to void the contents of my stomach).

An especially annoying or upsetting person might also be referred to as a "dry boak". In the medical or physical sense, a "dry boak" means retching, metaphorically it's a man or woman whose personality or conduct make them even more stomach churning than the average "boak".

A particularly upsetting incident of food poisoning, a stomach bug or perhaps overindulgence in the grain or the grape might result in an individual being so ill that uncontrolled and violent vomiting may occur. In such circumstances, someone might be said to be "boakin rings roon them" or even "boakin their guts up" or possibly "boakin their ring up"; what Billy Connolly and others have referred to as "talking to God on the Great White Telephone" i.e. having your head stuck down a toilet and uttering imprecations to the deity. Ok, nearly time for me dinner though I'm naw as hungry as I was, funny enough.

Scud

Not the Russian tactical ballistic missile, rather the Ulster Scots word "scud".

It shares some meanings with standard English, particularly those relating to speed or movement ("Scud aboot"; dash round aimlessly: "gan a quare scud"; probably travelling faster than is sensible) though not precisely the same usage ("scudding" clouds or the nautical term for sailing in a storm without any, or hardly any, sails).

In Ulster Scots, it can be used to signify a blow or a smack ("A hut him a quare scud"; I may have engaged in some necessary physical contact). Unrelated to any of these is perhaps its most common use, to denote a curse or bad luck.

When the scud is put on something, it's jinxed.

Often heard in betting parlours and sporting fields but useful in all circumstances where chance is a factor, any ill luck can be readily attributed to someone or something "putting a scud on it".
I hope that clarifies things for our Russian readers.

Bill and Coo

When we approach Valentine's Day every year, there a fair tae middlin' chance that young lovers o' all ages will be takin' their chance tae bill an coo tae their heart's content or as freely as circumstances will allow onyroad. However, to the Ulster Scot, a "coo" has an altogether different meaning, as, by the way, has "bill", but mair o' that anither day.

A "coo" is a cow, a general name for the mature female of a bovine animal but in Standard English can also mean the female of various other large animals, as the elephant or whale and informally, as disparaging and offensive slang, meaning a large, obese, and slovenly woman. The majority of these usages do not apply to Ulster Scots, particularly in light of the absence of whales, elephants and slovenly, obese women from everyday Ulster Scots life. The Ulster Scots "coo" (plural, coos or occasionally, kine) is one of the cornerstones of agricultural life, either for dairy farming ("milkin' coos") or beef cattle for the food industry.

Apart from milk, beef and leather, the coo's main output was dung, or coo-clap as Ulster Scots has it. After collecting said dung frae the byre and dumpin' it in the midden, it was spread over the arable land, either wae a shovel aff the back o' a trailer (scaling dung, not an activity for the weak of back or stomach) or latterly with the advent of mechanisation, a dung-spreader, a name as functional as it is poetic. There are philosophical points to be made in Ulster Scots referring to coo clap. "The mair ye tramp on a coo clap, the bigger ye mak it"; to rehash a messy incident serves only to make the mess bigger.

If a musician or singer of limited ability (or no ability at all) tackles a melody which highlights these shortcomings, the song or air is often described as "the tune the oul coo died to", not a flattering comparison but mair o'a reflection on the artist naw the tune.

Perhaps it's appropriate to mention at this point that Old Dobbin (or for that matter, Shergar) never featured as a menu item in Ulster Scots cuisine, either formally or informally.

Neigh chance!
The oul grey mare ain't what she used to be.
Apparently she's now lasagne.

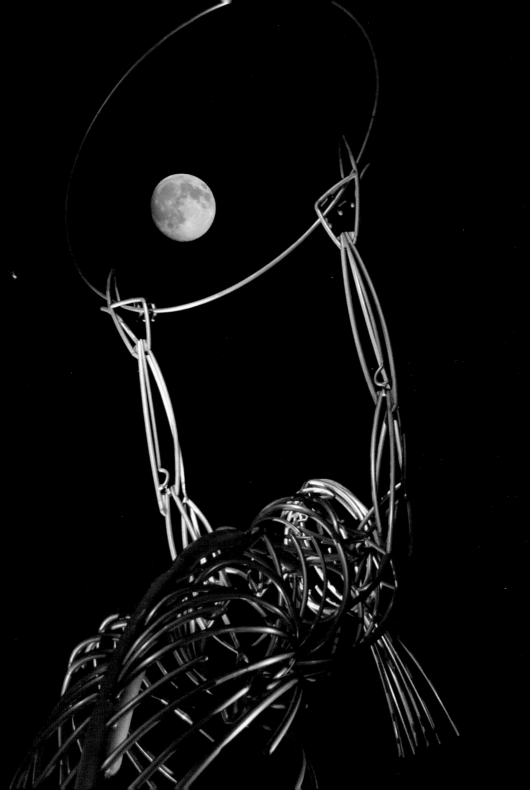

Up in Coort

Those Ulster Scots speakers with scant regard for the rules and organs of the state and prone to poor behaviour towards other citizens inevitably find themselves in close contact with the organized civil force for maintaining order and enforcing the laws. Or the Polis, as they are more commonly referred to. Any fans of televised Scandinavian crime fiction will recognise the Nordic origins of that name from the signs on the police (or polis) cars. While many interactions between the citizenry and the Peelers (English origin, long since abandoned there, still prevalent here) are dealt with informally (though I suspect the clash on the lug and boot up the erse of earlier days is no longer part of the community policing strategy), some offences were considered serious enough to be dealt with by the coorts. However, there are alternative meanings and it is these I am interested in today.

"Coort" to an Ulster Scot also means pitchin' woo, to pay court, to chase a mate, to search for Mr or Ms Right (or at least Mr or Ms Right Now). The silver tongued Ulster Scot is well practiced in the art of seduction and I offer a few classic examples of the rough-hewn romanticism which typifies these courtship rituals.

"What aboot a birl?" is an invitation to take the floor with a prospective partner. "Ye dinnae sweat much for a big girl" is a compliment to the fitness of your partner. An admiration for the figure of your dance partner might be indicated by saying "Ye hae the quare child bearin hips" or "Them's quare muscley thighs ye hae".

A lassie with a talent for the application of slap may be told "Ye're a dab han wae the make-up. Ye can hardly see yer moustache at aal".

Something tells me I might be coortin trouble. Daenae be getting the polis, noo.

Cope Carlie

The Standard English meaning of "cope" (to struggle with, deal with or to face up to responsibilities, problems, or difficulties, with some degree of success in a calm or adequate manner; we'll ignore the ecclesiastical and other meanings relating to building and falconry) is rarely used in Ulster Scots since we are such hardy and self-sufficient folk that the expectation is that we will deal with every situation in a successful manner, so much so that it doesn't merit much of a mention in everyday conversation.

"Cope" (or in some places "cowp") means to knock over or spill, demolish, fall or trip. So when someone tells you "Efter it was ower, I was fit tae cope", this doesn't indicate that the speaker was in a position to deal successfully with the aftermath of an event, rather it means that immediately after an incident, the person was so tired, they barely made it to the bed before falling fast asleep.

"They hae coped me oul school" means that my alma mater has been demolished.

"He run intae me that hard, A coped" (or "coped ower") indicates that our collision resulted in me landin on my erse.

"The reek o' 'im wus that bad, A near coped" conveys that the state of his personal hygiene was in such a poor state as to almost cause me to keel over. In gymnastics, a forward roll or somersault is known in Ulster Scots as a "cope carlie" but at my stage of life, I have executed my last cope carlie.

Craiter Comforts

Of the two main meanings for "craiter", it is difficult to pick which is the most prevalent since the two meanings enjoy no linguistic or literary connection that I can divine.

A "craiter" can be an individual (or an animal) who find themselves in an unfortunate or tragic set of circumstances who tends to naturally draw the sympathy and empathy of the onlooker, the bystander or the commentator, laik mesel.

"Craiter" carries an implication of guilelessness and purity ("he's an innocent craiter", "she's a harmless craiter", "the poor wee craiter") but there is also the possibility that the individual may be a ludicrous person or even a fool ("he's a silly craiter if he believes thon oul guff"; he would be well advised to be increase his intake of salt).

The other meaning relates to alcoholic beverages, or specifically, whiskey, either distilled by a professional manufacturer or created by an amateur, using a hillside still.

"A drap o' the craiter" (a tot or nip of whiskey) can be a cure for shock, a protection from the cold (coul), a celebratory tipple or as a medicinal remedy.

I'm a simple craiter wae a weakness for the craiter.
Perhaps I'm naw the only yin.

Deedle E D

There are two main meanings for "deedle", neither having any link to "deed" meaning dead.

A grandparent, a mum, a dad, an aunt or an uncle might "deedle" a wean on their knee though there is an age when deedlin stops. This could be due to the size, weight or age of the child or the state of the knees of the adult. The more common usage relates to speed of travel, whether on foot or in or on a contraption. People who deedle aren't in a rush, they have the time to smell the roses. ("He was deedlin alang the upper road in thon oul motor o' his wae nary a care in the worl"; the speed of his driving is such that, if caught behind him, you may be in danger of experiencing a cardiac episode) ("He come deedlin on thon bike"; his speed of cycling shouldn't trouble the Tour de France).

A worker accused of "deedlin" is usually not felt to be as enthusiastic about the task in hand as could reasonably be expected. It might be said of such an individual that "the deed lice was drappin aff him".

So maybe some slight connection between "deedle" and "deed". Not patient people the Ulster Scots, another of our many failings.

Shut thon Dour

Again with the spelling!

I've seen baith "dorr" and "dure" but my preference is for "dour".
The standard English "dour", with shared meaning, is applicable to the
Ulster Scot both in relation to demeanour and appearance ("He haes thon
oul dour face on him" I've seen him looking cheerier) or indeed the weather
("dour an dreech"; grey and depressing).

The Ulster Scots "dour" means "door" ("Shut thon dour" as an Ulster Scots
Larry Grayson might remark) but there are a number of variants on the
theme.

If a person "haes nae bak dours", this is generally a person to be trusted,
someone without a hidden agenda, an innocent abroad.

"Naw behin the dour" indicates a lack of shyness or timidity just a hair short
of rudeness, usually used in relation to food (what is sometimes called "the
lodger's reach") but applicable in a range of situations.

A gentleman, or for that matter a lady, who spends time visiting with
neighbours ("kailyin", from the Irish 'ceilidh') might be said "tae be roon the
dours" or a fruitless search might involve "gan roon the dours".
My favourite usage is employed by the inimitable W.F. Marshall in his poem
"Me an Me Da", often called "I'm livin in Drumlister".

When the protagonist of the piece is remarking on the ravages that smallpox
has wrought on a prospective soul mate, he comments,
"But her face was like a goal dour,
With the bowlts pult oot"

Naw behin the dour wae a smart remark was the Reverend Marshall, A
doot.

Wag the Doag

Certain words are recognised as geographic linguistic identifiers, their use
indicative of speech patterns and language usage in particular areas. So it
is with "doag" in Ulster Scots; meaning 'dog', the domestic pet. The use
of "doag" is usual in Ulster Scots speaking parts of the country. The Scots
mostly favour "dug" for 'dog 'and this usage can also be found in some parts
of Ulster but we are concerned today with "doag" and its usage in a number
of well used, and in some cases, well known, Ulster Scots phrases.

When a veteran is tasked with more responsible and onerous duties while
the novice, due to lack of experience or ability, tackles simpler matters, it
might be said that "the oul doag for the hard road and the pup for the pad",
"pad" being "path" in Ulster Scots.

"Not much heard outside of vintage tractor shows and ploughing matches, mechanical or horse powered, a description of a poorly ploughed furrow or drill might be "laik a doag pishin in the snow", in other words, crooked.

Friendships which blossom unexpectedly (and possibly in a manner which might be described as suspect) between parties who had previously not been on the best of terms could draw the comment "They wur at ither's throats naw lang ago, noo they're as big as doags' heids".

Folk who are able to chatter at length in a dull manner ("santer", "ganch" or "slabber") might be described as having the ability "tae tak a doag tae death"."

95

Drap in the Ocean

Part of my love of Ulster Scots is the vivid and imaginative way that words are used in not only their literal sense as well as their use in the creation of metaphors. "Drap" is a good case in point; as a verb and a noun, the shared meaning with the Standard English "drop" is clear enough.

No domestic social encounter would be complete without a "drap o tay", (see Mrs. Doyle), ether "in yer han" or "wae somethin tae taste yer mooth" (tea, without accompaniment or with a light snack).

It's the wider use which I like. If an individual is identified as being "fond o a drap", "taks a wee drap" or "laiks a drap", this refers to a fondness for a "drap o' the craiter", a man (or occasionally, a woman) with an over fondness for the bottle, especially whiskey. Such a person, in their cups or sober, may exhibit poor behavior, either bad manners or bad temper, and might be said to "hae a bad drap in them", probably a reference to bad blood or, in more modern parlance, bad genes. In order to emphasise the extent to which an individual "wae a bad drap in them" is unrelated to the speaker, they are described as "naw a drap's blid tae me", in other words, totally unrelated.

When people "drap aff", this is a reference to their demise whereas "drappin aff yer feet" just means dead tired.

In season, the arable farmer planting potatoes is said to be "drappin prootas" and the beef farmer, in season, hopes for "drapped" calves, new born calves.

A'm away tae hae a wee drap. Or maybe a brave drap.

Hut a Dunt

The more I think about it, the more it appears to me that Ulster Scots has a preponderance of words relating to physical contact. And very few of them are to do with the pleasanter side of physical contact, the vast majority relate to the less savoury aspects. "Dunt" fits rather neatly into this latter category.

Functioning as both a verb and a noun, "dunt" can mean nudge, thump, jab, poke, bump, prod, punch, push, shove or tap. ("I hut him a dunt he'll naw forget in a hurry"; I had occasion to physically chastise him in a manner which will live long in his memory).

There is an implication of noise with the dunt (I heerd a wile dunt ootside) in relation to inanimate objects which doesn't really apply when the reference is to a physical encounter between, say, sportsmen (He hut him a quare dunt when he tackled him; he dunted him that hard he went flyin'). A dunt can mean a minor vehicular collision, minor in the sense that the vehicle belongs to someone else, similar to a minor surgical operation i.e. one carried out on somebody else. So if someone has "a bit o' a dunt in the supermarket car park", we can be fairly sure that ownership of the vehicle in question lies somewhere other than with the speaker. Our American cousins might refer to such an encounter as a "fender bender".

Which reminds me, speaking of vehicle collisions, the fairground attraction referred to in most (but not all) English speaking jurisdictions as the dodgems are usually called "bumpin' cars" or "bumper cars" by the Ulster Scots, among others.

I am sure that tells us something about oursels.

Yer Erse an Parsley

One of my favourite words in Ulster Scots, "erse" equates to the Standard English "arse" meaning buttocks, bottom or a fool.

I have heard a few possible origins; the Old English "ærs" meaning tail or rump," there's Old Norse "ars" or Middle Dutch "ærs" even German "arsch", all meaning buttock. There's also possible Greek and Irish origins. But for me, the attraction is the rich variety of Ulster Scots expressions in which "erse" is employed.

Those of you unimpressed with my erudition or my intellect might be inclined to remark that "he knows as much about Ulster Scots as my erse knows about snipe-shootin", in other words, not a lot.

A poor quality footballer (or ball player of any stripe) may, on occasion, hear an onlooker exclaim "an oul woman wae a stray erse cud play better" and a failure to convert a scoring opportunity may draw the remark that the player "cudn't hit a bull on the erse wae a bakeboord" although I have heard this sentiment rendered in English as "couldn't hit a cow's arse (or a barn door) with a banjo".

There are a wide range of insults available to the Ulster Scot partial to the use of this multi-purpose word.

"Is yer eyes in yer erse" questions the eyesight of an individual as well as their powers of observation, a charge often levelled at referees. Such a referee may be deemed worthy of a swift physical chastisement, such as "a kick in the erse". This last is also a measure of proximity ("Was he close?" "He wasn't a kick in the erse aff it.")

The physical limits of endurance can be measured in terms of "as much as the erse can stan". Jim Fenton tells of the following exchange between long-winded preacher and a congregant. In response to an inquiry from the cleric whether she had enjoyed the sermon, she replied "Aye mine this, yer reverence: the heid can only tak in as much as the erse can stan". Allow me to apply that lesson to myself.

Moonlight Flit

For those of a certain age, "flit" (or actually "Flit") is a word closely associated with the war on insects, particularly the fly and the bluebottle, since "Flit" was a branded product, an insecticide spray used freely in the days before we were afraid of DDT or depletion of the ozone layer. If memory serves, and it rarely does these days, there may have a been a Flit gun to zap our six legged enemies.

The Ulster Scots word "flit" (also used in the North of England) means to move home, to relocate. Some may be familiar with the expression "a Seterday flit's a short sit"; in other words, if you move on a Saturday, there is a strong possibility you won't remain in your new place of residence for very long. Whatever the validity of this old wives tale, I am aware that hospitals are usually reluctant to sanction Saturday discharges though whether this is due to a belief in the saying or relates more to administrative practice in hospitals is a matter of conjecture.

Those who are in a quandary as to whether a change of address (or a change of circumstance) will materially improve their circumstances are referred to the saying "Better rue sit as rue flit" meaning there are more advantages (or rather, less disadvantages) to staying where you are, physically or metaphorically, rather than making a wrong move which may not be so easily put right.

A moonlight flit (an expression heard occasionally in Standard English) means to depart secretly, often leaving unresolved issues such as rent and other bills. Done the odd time by the odd Ulster Scot.

An Oul Flooster

The Ulster Scot doesn't really go in for extravagant shows of emotion. Truth to be told, even not so extravagant displays aren't much in evidence either. In fact, they are actively discouraged, the Ulster Scot favouring the undemonstrative, frugal with emotional displays, dare I say, laconic. Laconic comes from the Greek area of Laconia, which contained Sparta and the Spartans are famous for their unemotional approach to life, their dust dry humour and their economy with words. They were also known for being brave an' fightable.

Which brings us to our word, "flooster".

There is a shared meaning with the Standard English word "fluster" meaning agitated confusion, nervous excitement, upset or bewilderment ("He's aye getting himsel floostered"; he is prone to poor performance under pressure). In my youth, to be described as a "flooster" was to be identified as someone inclined to excessive displays of emotion, displays which were suspect, whose honesty and truthfulness was in question. The exchange of "air kisses" represents the very embodiment of being a "flooster". Crocodile tears, impassioned declarations of devotion and gestures of affection are all dismissed as "floosterin" ("Quet your oul floosterin"; desist from your false histrionics, they are cutting no ice with me).

To be known as a flooster is to be regarded as false, someone who flatters to deceive, whose kisses carry all the love and devotion of Judas.

I can see so many similarities between the Spartans and the Ulster Scots.

Fog It Intae Ye

Handy at times of festive overeating such as Christmas, our word is "fog". Yes it means a mist, same as English (tiny drops of condensed water vapour suspended in air, reducing visibility, a cloud at a lower level, to be scientific), and it can also be used to describe lichen or moss on stone but for the festive season, we'll focus on its use in relation to eating and drinking.

"He fogged it in 'im" suggests an enthusiastic eater, perhaps even an overenthusiastic eater.

Many may have been "foggin an eating" a Christmas dinner in them on the day but "foggin an eatin" tae mae ain mine, implies a bit of gluttony. The same meaning can be achieved using "gorb".

And surely we're not all gluttons an gorbs?

Fog it in ye onyroad.

Footer Aboot

Footer means (verb) to work with something to no obvious effect or in an unenthusiastic or slapdash way (He done naethin but footer wae it) (Quet footerin an dae somethin wae it)

Footer (noun) someone who works or behaves ineffectively or ineffectually (Dinnae let him near it, he's only a footer)

Origin: from medieval French futre meaning the physical act of love
Also used in the expression "a left footer" indicating someone of a different religious persuasion but this meaning is unrelated to the other meanings detailed here.

Gether Yer Thoughts

When in 2009 Kate Winslet won her second Golden Globe, awarded best actress for her role in the film Revolutionary Road, she famously calmed herself by exclaiming "Gather! Gather!". She couldn't have confused them more had she said "Gether". Equating pretty closely to the standard English "gather", so collecting potatoes becomes "getherin prootas". Can also be used to describe a motley crew, a crowd of people held in little regard, a "gether up".

To frown or scowl (the English "scowl" in this instance, not the Ulster Scots "scowl" which means to scold or complain) can be described as "getherin the broos"; to quote Burns' Tam O'Shanter, "Gethering her broos like gethering storm" describing a wife awaiting the return of an errant husband.

An encouragement to straighten up and fly right or simply sort yourself out might be "gether yersel thegither".

Kate eventually "gethered hersel thegither".

Gleek an Ye'll Find

If someone (an Ulster Scots speaker), wants a quick look, a peep or a peek, they might say "Gie us a gleek". Should the request be acceded to, they could then be said to have had a "gleek" or possibly, if some importance were attached to the observation, they might say "I only had a quick gleek"; the period of observation was so fleeting as to render it almost meaningless. Peeping Tom, that ungallant resident of Coventry, was said to have spied on Lady Godiva as she paraded naked through the city. Even though he maintained all he had was a wee gleek through the hole he'd bored in his window shutter, he was deemed to have had an eyeful and was struck blind for his troubles.

People have been known, on occasion, to ask for a "duke" at something but this is not really a true Ulster Scots expression. It is instead a reference to Geoffrey Ernest Duke OBE, better known as Geoff Duke, a man who became the first motorcycling superstar and a byword for speedy riding or driving (if stopped by the Polis for exceeding the speed limit, a driver might be asked if they thought they were Geoff Duke). This became a sort of rhyming slang expression, a Geoff Duke being a glance, a peek, a look. Although it might have been used by Ulster Scots among many others, given our historic and continuing love affair with the motorbike, it is a sort of faux Cockney.

Of coorse, there is a "jook" in Ulster Scots but we'll hae a gleek at that anither time.

Gowl at the Moon

To some extent, the Ulster Scot enjoys a reputation for stoicism, an ability to endure the cruellest of life's bitter blows without a flicker of emotion, to meet success and remain unmoved. There is, of coorse, mair nor a grain o' truth in this belief but rather laik the boy that gets a name for early risin' but aye lies tae dinnertim, the reality disnae allus square wae the legend.

The Ulster Scot can be heard to "gowl" (cry out, cry, shout, basically any loud noise) in a number of circumstances; a good or a bad football result can stimulate gowlin', or indeed for that matter, greetin' (weeping, crying, tearful behaviour) and during the course of a season or a tournament, gowlin an greetin are a commonplace occurrence, certainly more frequent than the reputation might lead you to expect ("He let a gowl oot o 'im would a deefened ye").

Weddings, funerals, births and departure lounges of most stripes are usually accompanied by a certain amount of gowlin, aye, an nae shortage o' greetin ether.

The gowl can also be a measure of distance or accuracy but we employ a specific gowl as a measuring tool. That gowl belongs to the baigle, known in Standard English as a beagle, a breed with a reputation for smoking rather than hunting or for that matter, gowling. I'm pretty sure that Snoopy from the Peanuts cartoon strip is a baigle or a beagle.

If something "wasnae within a baigle's gowl" of something else, this is an indication of either geographic inaccuracy, a location being sought, say, or general inaccuracy, such as a poor guess or estimate.

It is my fervent hope that this piece comes within a baigle's gowl of capturing the word's meanings.

If not, quet yer greetin.

The Grape of Wrath

We Ulster Scots speakers use the word "grape" in exactly the same way as Standard English, for instance "Beulah, peel me another grape" though that phase was famously coined by the actress Mae West and is not much heard among native speakers o' the hamely tongue.

The grape, fruit of the vine, legitimate part of your five-a-day (but only in its unfermented state), progenitor of the raisin, the sultana and alcoholic beverages ranging from Buckie (as Buckfast Fortified Wine is known to its aficionados) to brandy, has a whole other additional meaning to the Ulster Scot.

I am a great admirer of Larne's John Clifford, a poet, playwright, author, thespian and founder of the Larne and District Folklore Society and there is a story told of his time in London as a jobbing actor. As almost anyone possessed of an Equity card will tell you, there can be long (unpaid) intervals between engagements (or resting, as it is known in the trade). Many actors (though not all) use this time for gainful employment of a casual nature and Clifford augmented his acting income with some gardening.

In order to better discharge his horticultural endeavours, he went to a hardware shop in Kensington and asked for a grape. Not here mate, he was told, you need a greengrocer. Clifford then explained that his grape had a wooden handle and three or four metal prongs. Oh, cried the hardware man, you mean a gardening fork!

Which was correct but grossly underestimates the wide variety of uses the grape was put to, particularly reddin' out (cleaning out) byres and scaling (spreading) dung.

The word also features in one of my absolute favourite Ulster Scots expressions. An individual with no redeeming features whatsoever and a preference for the underhand and the crooked would inevitably be given the character reference "A nicer fella ye cudn't stick a grape in".

Always ready with a kind word, the Ulster Scot.

Gunk in Charge

The Ulster Scot speaker is a hardy soul. There is very little can upset the equilibrium of the man or woman with Scotch Irish heritage. However, a rare event is one which may not happen often, but it does happen, so we are not totally immune to shock, agitation, dismay, upset or trouble.

When such an unusual event does occur, the Ulster Scot is said to be "gunked" or might equally well be described as having had a "gunk". A "gunk" can be a blow to your pride, disappointment in a loved one, a friend's betrayal, incompetence or unkindness, a shock of any kind, perhaps even a favourable shock.

In any event, an individual has been taken aback at what has occurred. There are of course gradations of gunk; a particularly nasty or unexpected turn of events can be best described as a "quare gunk" and the recipient of such a "quare gunk" might be said to be "badly gunked".

On the positive side of things, the Ulster Scot is nothing if not resilient. So while we are, on the odd occasion, subject to gunks, quare or otherwise, rather like a boxer on the receiving end of a sudden left hook or an unforeseen uppercut, we shake wur heids, grit wur teeth an come oot swinging.

Gye Laik the Thing

I was on the internet recently and read an Ulster Scots feature which told me with some authority that the Ulster Scots word "gye" meant "very". Jest houl yersel there a minute. Yer naw right, at least, naw completely.

"Gye" is a modifier or an intensifier, a word that indicates, and usually increases, the degree of emphasis or force to be given to the word it modifies or intensifies. One of those senses is "very", there nae doot about it but there a lock mair tae "gye "than "very".

A part of a better definition might be "considerable" or "considerably" ("gye lang"; "gye big") and these phrases might equally well be rendered as "gye an lang" or "gye an big".

If a thing is partly or largely complete, it can be said to be "gyely dane" (of a task) or "gyely ower" (of a shower of rain).

The question "How are ye daein?" might draw the response "A'm daein gyely" (I'm as well as might be expected under the circumstances).
If confronted with a good approximation of something or a plausible substitute or alternative, an Ulster Scot might remark "It's gye laik the thing" or even "it's gye an laik the thing".

A dae hope this definition of "gye" is gye an laik the thing.

Oul Han

Naethin tae dae wae the Han dynasty that ruled China for four hundred years, "han" is the Ulster Scots rendition of the Standard English word "hand". To describe someone as a "dab han" is to compliment them for their expertise or skill although this can be turned to an insult, "a dab han at naethin" meaning useless. This can also be rendered as a "bad han".

A "sore han" or a "sad han" means that an event or an endeavour has been dealt with incompetently or bungled entirely ("They hae made a sad han o' thon extension"; their building project has been clumsily executed). This may be because either the owners (if they are doing it themselves) or their builder are "hanless", lacking in skill or dexterity or they "hae hans for naethin". Perhaps they aren't capable of "daein a han's turn".
Perhaps they should have employed an "oul han", a veteran or long serving individual with the necessary skills. "Oul han" can also mean "friend" in a friendly sense or friend in an unfriendly sense ("Luk, oul han, this haes naethin tae dae wae ye, so mine yer ain business" ; "Could I kindly suggest that it might be in your best interest to pay no further attention to this matter").

If a substantial inheritance or a windfall, like a lottery win, is not utilised to best effect, seasoned observers of life might comment that "it taks a steady han tae houl a full cup". A happy turn of events or change of circumstances might alter a situation so that it suited you better. Such an advantage means that matters might consequently "lie tae yer han". If such matters are to be dealt with successfully, they must be "tuk in han".

If you are teased, your tormentors are said to be "takkin the han oot o' ye". You might respond by saying "the bak o' me han tae ye" (we are no longer friends) or possibly by applying physical force ("A tuk the bak o' me han tae him"; I chastised him).

An all too common course of action for the Ulster Scot.

Hannle Yersel

The Standard English word "handle" is almost directly equivalent to the Ulster Scots "hannle" as both verb and noun, sharing most or at least many of the meanings.

However, there are a couple of examples of use specifically within Ulster Scots. Although widely used during the height of the CB radio boom, a person on the air might use a special CB name, a "hannle", but this is from the home of CB radio, the United States, where handle is the accepted term for this practice.

A person with a gift for pugilism (the art or practice of fighting with one's fists or boxing) would generally be recognised as someone who could "hannle themsels". Such an individual might be said to be "handy wae their mitts".

If someone were to find themselves in what the Americans describe as a situation and we would call a quandary, perhaps even an argument, a row or a dilemma, the Ulster Scot may call this a "hannlin". An individual with a contrary nature (many Ulster Scots fall into this category) could be said to be capable of "startin a hannlin in an empy hoose".

If ever caught in this type of circumstance, it is advantageous "tae be fit tae hannle yersel". And if this happened to be a particularly trying, challenging or tricky hannlin, it could be said to be "sum hannlin".

Het an Reekin

There is a Standard English word, "het", to heat up or heated, which is, of course, very close indeed to the Ulster Scots meaning. However, in English it is an archaic term; in Ulster Scots it is still very much alive and in common(ish) usage.

"Het" means hot, whether in connection with temperature ("A gye het day"; a reference to the weather rarely heard in ordinary speech) or metaphorical (Whun he finally got the houl o her, he gin it tae her het an reekin; after a small delay, he eventually chastised her as severely as the situation demanded).

If people go at a thing "het stitch", this can indicate that it is undertaken without undue delay and/or without inhibition. If a couple were described as bein at it "het stitch", this could either indicate they were arguing or courting, depending on their age and the stage of their relationship.

A recalcitrant or cheeky child, who might be identified as being in need of a minor physical chastening could be said to "need his erse weel het", in other words, in want of a little physical punishment.

Although nowadays, in times of political correctness, this could be said to be a grey area.

Hirple Aboot

There are two main uses of "hirple", the more accurate and serious use is a reference to a limp and the hobbling walk adopted by those thus afflicted ("He hirpled roon laik he only had yin guid leg" He wasn't as supple as he might have been)("He haes a quare hirple" He's not good on his feet due to his limp).

Those inclined to "hirple" might be old or physically afflicted or simply ungainly.

This last gives rise to the other use of "hirple", as a term of abuse aimed at those not moving as speedily or freely or as gracefully as they might, particularly sportsmen of all codes who aren't playing or performing at an optimum level.

This may be due to injury or indeed age or for that matter, a lack of skill or ability.

A footballer, rugby player or hurler might be described as "hirplin roon laik an oul woman, in other words, not playing well at all.

It might also be applicable to any worker, where movement is part of the job, who is performing below par.

One of the reasons for hirplin may be the possession of a "hilsh", a permanent limp. I am indebted to Jim Fenton for the tale of the meeting between his parents and those of his bride to be, good Belfast stock. This meeting took place at a time when Jim's father, Sam, was recovering from a leg injury which reduced his mobility.

As they departed, Jim's prospective in-laws wished Sam a speedy recovery. "As lang as A haenae a hilsh" he replied.

He's a Hobbledehoy

I was pleasantly surprised the other week while watching "Downton Abbey" to hear a good Ulster Scots word make an appearance in the script. The long-suffering butler, Mr. Carson (a name with many resonances on this side o' the sheugh), played by the estimable actor Jim Carter, exasperated at the staff cutbacks being experienced at the Abbey, declared his unwillingness to train a group of "hobbledehoys".

Let me say straight out that I am claiming neither Carson nor Julian Fellowes (the author of DA) as Ulster Scots or Ulster Scots speakers but that word was widely used in Ulster Scots speaking areas.

Carson (or Fellowes) meant it in the sense I am familiar with, raw youth just at the start of adult life, inexperienced, naive, gullible. My late grandmother had an expression of utter derision which not only belittled the individual being spoken about but also provided a succinct definition of the word. "He's a hobbledehoy, nether a man nor a boy" was a damning character summary and one not always applied exclusively to young people.

The term is an archaic one in Standard English, from Elizabethan times meaning a clumsy or awkward youth. The first element "hob" is probably in the sense of "clown, prankster" (for instance hobgoblin); the second element seems to be Medieval French, "de haye" meaning "worthless, untamed, wild," literally "of the hedge".

Sadly my hobbledehoy days are far behind me.

My Lovely Horse

I should really apologise given the food scares but sadly I cudnae resist since "horse" is a guid Ulster Scots word wae its ain meaning to Ulster Scots people.

Many of its meanings are shared with Standard English, particularly references to the big, solid-hoofed, herbivorous quadruped, (Equus caballus) domesticated frae prehistoric times, bred in a wheen o' varieties, and used for carrying or pulling loads, for riding or racing and more recently, as a tasty addition to our local cuisine.

Aye, a chippy whiles haes yin for workin on, the carpenter chippy that is, naw the purveyor o deep fried bits o prootas an ither treats. If ye fool aroon, a boady could be said tae be horsin aboot.

If an Ulster Scot gets a promise that their circumstances should improve tomorrow, if not sooner, this might draw the sarcastic response "live, oul horse, an you'll get grass". In other words, jam tomorrow.

An if ye want a boady tae stap or slow doon or quet what they're daein, ye wud say "houl yer horses". There mony a yin that was niver near a bookie's or a racetrack that haes backed the wrang horse (even when they got their information straight frae the horse's mooth) an mony a yin that niver had a whip in their han but haes put a lock o effort intae flogging a dead horse. When the Ulster Scot is hungry ("able tae ate a man aff his horse" or even, "ate a horse") or if the time allowed for eating is limited or should there be fierce competition at the table (there were eight or nine roon oor dinner table when I was wee so if ye didnae eat quick, ye didnae eat), they might go at it enthusiastically and could be said to be "horsin' it intae them". Alternatively, a good host might encourage guests to "horse it intae yes". Perhaps not so much after recent events.

Ill Met by Moonlight

The Ulster Scot speaker uses "ill" in a sense that dates from Elizabethan times and remains in Standard English both as a prefix (ill at ease, ill-fated, ill-starred) and as a noun (daenae speak ill o' the dead) as well as an adverb (an expense we can ill afford) but there are a number of specific uses, unique to Ulster Scots.

The origins are supposedly Old Norse, meaning bad, and while it is possible that "ill" might be used by the Ulster Scot in the context of health (or the lack thereof), more often it's use is in a range of Ulster Scots meanings, many harking back to that original Norse usage.

"Ill tae work wae" could refer to a work colleague but is more often used about an encounter with an awkward individual (not such a rara avis in Ulster Scots' circles) which has been hard work ("He's ill tae work wae cause he's that thran"; that stubborn streak he possesses means he requires careful handling).

Similarly, a smug or superior attitude (also rare in Ulster Scots) can be said to be "ill tae stan" or "ill tae thole". For instance, poorly considered or cruel remarks about one's football team could be ill tae stan.

The recipient of such bantering might feel that people were being hard on them or "Ill on" ("They were gye ill on the manager efter thon batin"; the manager received some harsh criticism after a recent defeat). Those who don't care for that particular managerial regime could be said to be "naw ill bout thon boady".

The problem might be the wages bill, since the modern sportsman is "ill tae pie" (expensive or greedy or both), or possibly the manager is ill daein (throwing money about foolishly). Perhaps the coaching methods are not proving successful, the players are "ill tae learn", hard to teach.

Supporters who possess less manners than the norm, possibly due to a poor upbringing (ill bred) might accuse their opponents, or their supporters, of being ill-lukkin. Such an "ill lukkin" individual may confound the expectations of the non-native speaker by appearing as healthy as a horse but it is the possession of an ugly countenance that makes them "ill lukkin".

Such people are said to be "ill tongued" (The man or woman who is deemed to be "ill tongued" is nearly always ready with an insult, usually something barbed and cruel) and those displeased by such behaviour might "tak ill wae it".

An expensive tradesman can be "ill tae pie".

"Ill" is infrequently used in the medical sense though people who fall sick can, on occasion, be said to "hae tuk ill".

However, when someone "taks ill wae" with a person or a situation, they are usually finding that they don't like the individual or the circumstances. There is a strange contradiction in that if you are "ill on" something ("ill on a wean", of a parent or a teacher, "ill on petrol", of a vehicle), you are hard on the child or fuel; if you are "ill agin", you are deeply opposed (the Ulster Scot being deeply opposed to most things) but if you are "ill aboot" a person or an object, you are fond, admiring, perhaps even amorous.

And of course, there is that rare Ulster Scot, the man, woman or child who has nae manners.

Such people are judged to be ill rared or ill bred ("an ill-rared whelp"; "an ill bred skitter").

I always say, naebdy can help the way they were rared.

I trust this won't inspire any of you to "tak ill agane me".

By the Holy Jakers

"Jakers" is a rather strange word. For a start, it would occasionally be rendered as "Japers". But whether "Jakers" or "Japers", it is widely used in Ulster Scots as a mild exclamation of surprise or emotion ("Jakers, ye surprised me there" "Jakers, A can hardly believe thon's him").

There are a couple of minor variants, all equally applicable to either spelling or pronunciation. The use of "by", by way of an intensifier, making its use rather oath-like is common ("By Jakers, I'll sort this oot yince an fer aal"; I am determined to resolve this matter satisfactorily). Another adaptation, also emphasising the oath like nature of the word, is the addition of Holy as a prefix ("Holy Jakers"; "by the Holy Jakers").

The explanation (rather than definition) of "Jakers" to which I am most attracted is as a euphemism for the Lord's name, often rendered in Ulster Scots as "Jaysus" by those less concerned with the use of profanity.

There's a North American legacy to this Ulster Scots word, still in use there today as a mild exclamation of surprise or emotion or indeed as a euphemism. "Jakers" and "Japers" crossed the Atlantic and became "Jeepers", "by Jeepers" and "Holy Jeepers".

"Jeepers Creepers" whether as an ejaculation or a movie or song title, is authentically North American, naethin tae dae wae us, by Jakers.

Lowse Yersel

While it has an obvious connection to the standard English loose or loosen, there is no link to lose or losing.

It can mean untie, unhitch or unfasten (lowse them horses; lowse thon rope) and is the direct opposite of yock which, as you may have guessed, means tie, hitch or fasten. No relationship either, to the head louse or any of the other lousy lice which may afflict the Ulster Scot.

An Ulster Scots man's response to a call of nature might involve the "lowsin o a button", the opening of a fly, in preparation for blessed relief. This has been reduced in usage, in part due to a redesign of breeks which replaced the button fly with the zipper as well as the introduction of indoor plumbing, since "lowsin a button" was essentially an outdoor activity.

If a couple were bent on marriage when both were of, shall we say, a more mature age than ordinarily associated with that institution, people might have said of them "They're yockin whun they should be lowsin". No translation required!

The end of the working day might also be referred to as "lowsin time", time tae unyock the horses and danner home wae yer work daen. Laik mesel.

Weel Mended

The Ulster Scot is not usually associated with subtlety or understatement but there are instances when a delicate touch, linguistically speaking, is the favoured option. The expression employing "mended" heard most often is the remark that a person is "well mended" or "weel mended". This can be applied to an individual successfully recuperating from an illness or recovering from a health issue and is, on occasion, heard in this context.

The more subtle, and more common, use is to indicate that an individual (there is no distinction made in this regard between male and female) has been over attentive to the biscuit box, the cake tin or the sweet trolley and is consequently carrying some additional, the cruel might say excess, poundage.

"Boysadears but yer weel mended" may sound innocent, indeed even complimentary, but don't be fooled. A rough approximation in Standard English might be "My God, look at the size of you!".

The clear implication to the Ulster Scot is "You're as big as a hoose" and begs the question " Daes yer jaws iver stap chowin?" (You've grown to a considerable size and I wondered if your mouth ever stops moving?). Those with this predilection for "stuffin their bake" are not unknown in Ulster Scots circles and we have a couple of words which we use to identify these folk. A "gorb" or more often, a "greedy gorb", is just such an individual as is a "glunterpudden" although the glunterpudden is stupid as well as morbidly obese.

So, if someone says "You're weel mended", bear in mind what's in their mind and get yersel away tae Slimming World or doon the gym.

Fut in Mooth

There's a straight read across from the Ulster Scots "mooth" and the Standard English "mouth" but we use it in a range of phrases which render it wur ain.

A generous host would "gie ye the bite oota their mooth" whereas a less than hospitable one "wudnae let on ye had a mooth on ye", the difference between one who keeps a good table and one who doesn't. A tasty bite to accompany a beverage or to give added relish to an otherwise bland meal could be said to "taste yer mooth".

If a person is described as "burdmoothed", this indicates someone so timid and tongue-tied as to be unable to speak up for themselves, "naw able tae open their mooth". It is often used in the negative ("She's naw yin bit burdmoothed", said of an assertive female, happy to share her views with the world).

Those with loud voices, strong opinions or indiscreet natures may be said to be "big o the mooth" and if they are in the habit of imposing their company where it's not welcome, they could be said to be "sittin in yer mooth".

On those rare occasions when the Ulster Scot employs what has been described as "industrial language" (a string of expletives), usually after a mishap with a tool, such as hitting your thumb with a hammer, or if a horse, in which he had a financial interest, performs significantly below expectations, they are said to "come oot wae a moothfa".

Such behaviour can, in certain circumstances, earn the offender an instantaneous sanction, such as a slap in the mooth.

Not a Myowt

While I am favouring Jim Fenton's spelling, I do recognise a difficulty with getting the spelling and hence the pronunciation, spot on.

A "myowt" is a small sound but especially a (small) word of argument or rebuttal, thus when an opponent is bested in an argument or a debate, they are said to be bereft of a response, which would be rendered as "there wasnae anither myowt oot o him (or her!)".

A common admonishment to a recalcitrant or disobedient child, particularly one given to noisy protest when confronted with an instruction from an authority figure, would be "Naw a myowt oota ye" or possibly "Naw yin mair myowt oota ye", depending on whether the argument had started or not and the extent to which any debate had developed. Generally Ulster Scots parent/offspring argument is kept to a bare minimum, usually starting after the child has turned thirty or has developed sufficient physicality to render the outcome of any confrontation doubtful.

If a confrontation has rendered the position of an opponent untenable or at least difficult, the retelling of the episode would inevitably end with "he hadn't a myowt", representing a total victory.

Similarly, where there is an element of shame provoked ("I asked her whur she'd been an who she was wae an there wasnae a myowt").
Like so many Ulster Scots words, there is some debate as to the origin.
One school of thought has it as a variant of a Scots word "moot" meaning whisper or hint while others link it to "mot" and "gemot" an Old and Middle English by way of Old German and Old Low Frankish meaning discussion/meeting.

Nae metter, if there a myowt oota ony o' yes, it'll naw bother me yin iota.

Near the Mark

Laik wur cousins ower the sheugh, the Ulster Scot enjoys a reputation for being careful with money, careful to the point of being known as "near". "Near" means tight-fisted, parsimonious, stingy or miserly. This isn't as bad a term of abuse as might be thought since we take a certain amount of pride in managing our finances to good effect. Nevertheless, most people would be reluctant to hear themselves described "a boady as near as I iver met" or indeed "as near as nixt dour". This can also be rendered as "nearbegan".

There are other uses which chime more with the Standard English usage. The slapdash, lazy or sly worker will be familiar with all the short cuts associated with a task, these can be described as "near cuts". This can also be applied to a navigator.

The geographical location of a place can be close ("nearhan") or closer ("nearderhan") or oot o the way ("Naw yin bit nearhan").
Those who take risks which result in proximity to danger, trauma or punishment might be said to be "near themsels".

For a Newance

When an unexpected or unusual event takes place or an unprecedented series of events occurs, this is described in Ulster Scots as a "newance". ("It's a newance for him tae be oot as late as this"; It's not usual for him to be up at this hour:).

"For newance" or "For a newance" can also be something suggested for a change, for variety, such as attendance at a hostelry ("We'll take a run up tae thon new place, for a newance") or a destination ("We'll tak a rin doon tae the Port, for newance").

If an individual normally noted for poor housekeeping skills takes a sudden urge to spring-clean, it might be said, when the Ulster Scots equivalent of Kim and Aggie cast a cold eye over the premises, that "The hoose wasnae lukkin laik a tip, for a newance".

It can also be used to refer to a turn of events totally out of keeping with the norm. ("When it come his turn tae stan a roun, he pit his han in his poaket, laik an ordinary boady, for newance"; "He's normally noted for his parsimonious ways but in this instance, he was as generous as one would expect from anybody").

That's enough of a newance for now.

In Tae the Oxters

On occasion, "oxter" can be rendered as "uxter" but with no variation in meaning. It means armpit or armpits, or as wur American freens hae it, the pits, although the American version (or at least the slang version) carries the additional meaning of an extremely disagreeable or unpleasant, boring, or depressing place, condition or person.

If an individual is involved closely in something, usually something bad, they are said to be "in it tae the oxters" or "up tae their oxters", a phrase which really needs no translation but which is, of course, a metaphor. The phrase derives from the moss (a bog or swamp) and refers to stepping into soft ground and sinking to the depth of your oxters; a messy situation, literally or metaphorically.

If a person is carried or helped to walk by catching them under the arms, this manoeuvre is the oxter cog, usually employed on people rendered infirm by old age, illness or overindulgence in (normally) refreshing alcoholic beverages.

It may be a surprise to some but the Ulster Scots can be aware of the potential anti-social impact of the oxter on the nostrils of others. I am reminded of the farmer who wished to improve his personal hygiene and to that end, went to his local pharmacy in search of odoriferous unguents or anti-perspirant, if you prefer. Having established his requirements, the pharmacist asked him for his preference. "Ball or aerosol?".

"Neither" replied our hero "I wanted it for me oxters".

Only a Piesle

One of my favourite Ulster Scots terms of abuse, and there is an extremely wide range to choose from, is "piesle".

While some words have not only survived but thrived and passed into common usage among non-Ulster Scots speakers (girn, slabber and ganch spring to mind), "piesle" has lain at least partially hidden from common speech. What does it mean?

Well it's nae compliment!

"Piesle" is both noun and verb, you can both piesle ("He haes daen naethin only piesle aboot"; his methods and work rate haven't been as effective as might have been hoped) as well as being a piesle, a clumsy and ineffectual worker and therefore, a person of little note.

Its main function is to express dissatisfaction with the efforts of another. The underpinning word it calls to my mind is weak, "piesle" indicates a person of little or no physical substance and by inference, little worth. A "piesle", if they do anything at all, will be liable to footer with things or pintle aboot rather than get it sorted out.

To quote James Fenton from his "The Hamely Tongue", "Did ye iver in a' yer days see sitch a bit o' pintlin an pieslin?".

Did he mean me or you?

A Quare Guid Rairin

Naethin tae dae wae scarcity, infrequency or style of cooking (anything emerging from the pan short of burnt is deemed raw in Ulster Scots cuisine), "rair" has a number of meanings in Ulster Scots, equating in broad terms to some of the Standard English meanings of "rear".

How you were brought up is how ye were raired. A person with a substandard upbringing may be judged to be "only half raired", possibly even "mair dragged up nor raired".

A particularly objectionable or dislikable individual may be adjudged to be so deplorable that even the parents may not hold a high opinion of their offspring, or as we say in Ulster Scots, "ye cudnae laik them if ye raired them".

If a person "raired up" or "rairs up", this indicates that the individual concerned has taken umbrage with something and vents their objection noisily. And of course, the average Ulster Scot usually takes umbrage with such enthusiasm that they are deemed "rairin to go", a meaning shared with Standard English.

An amount of money, either paid out, wasted or lost (loast), is usually diminished in importance by being identified as insufficient to have (or have had) a major impact on domestic life; in Ulster Scots "it niver raired us".

A better go before somebody rairs up.

Redd Up the Pedigrees

Not the colour and unrelated to literary matters, the closest standard English word to "redd" would be "rid" meaning to free, relieve or unencumber but as so often in Ulster Scots, it carries additional layers of meaning. An extravagant spending spree might mean "reddin the purse".

An infraction of discipline or etiquette might result in the offending party getting "redd up" or recieveing a "reddin up", meaning a few (or more) harsh words.

A poor worker might be "got redd o" or sacked.
If two or more are gathered together (or "gethered thegither") to gossip about an individual and his or her wider family circle, they are said to be "reddin up the pedigrees".

Those wanting something emptied or cleared or those anxious to bring matters to a close might be said to want things "redd up".
Laik mesel.

A Rickle o Bones

To the older Ulster Scot, one familiar with rural life, "rickle" has a place in the life-cycle of the peat; to "rickle" means to place (almost dry) peats in small piles for the final drying, prior to puttin them into the stack, the stack being the last resting place before consignment to the fire. The small piles created are referred to as rickles. These structures are open and as unstable as one might expect since there is little regularity in the shape and size of the peats (think of the latter stages of a game of Jenga using irregular blocks). A house in poor order, to use the language of the estate agent, requiring significant refurbishment, could be described as a rickle ("How he lives in thon oul rickle o a hoose in the winter is beyond me"; the poor state of repair of his main dwelling place must make the winters very hard).

Similarly, a car (more often referred to as a motor) requiring the ministrations of the mechanic and the body shop will be identified as an "oul rickle o a motor". Not quite so many of these nowadays, mainly thanks to the tireless work of the constabulary and the relevant government departments but once upon a time, a man in a rural setting was discovered driving his oul rickle down the main road in reverse, a strategy he had adopted when all his forward gears failed some seven months previously. He had gone undetected for all that time. Not very likely nowadays.

If a person or for that matter, an animal, is deemed to be undernourished or at least not as well-fed (or as generously proportioned) as might be expected, they might be described as a "rickle o bones".

As a youth, I was a rickle o bones but I'm a more substantial citizen the day or if you prefer, I'm naw yin bit rickly.

Rummle Aboot

"Rummle" is a very flexible Ulster Scots word, useful as a verb and a noun. There are some similarities with the Standard English "rumble"; inclement weather (such a rarity in wur ain wee country) can on occasion mean the presence of a thunderclap or a "rummle o' thunner" although "rummle" in this context indicates there is some distance from the centre of the storm. Closer and it would be a brattle o thunner.

If a person "rummles through" this can either indicate overcoming challenging personal circumstances ("A daenae know if A'll be fit tae rummle through"; I'm not sure I'll be able to cope with this situation) or a search undertaken in an informal manner ("A got her rummlin through the cupboards" I came upon her engaged in a search of the storage cabinets). A "rummlin o the guts" may indicate extreme hunger (a constant problem for the Ulster Scot) or perhaps the presence of a surfeit of wind within the digestive tract (another recurrent difficulty for the Ulster Scot).

Personally, my preferred use is the term "rummly" (as in "He's a rummly cove"; he's an individual worth keeping a good eye on: or "They're a rummly lock o boadies"; the whole lot of them are worth a watching) meaning untrustworthy, capricious and unpredictable.

To be fair it's rarely used, there being such a shortage of Ulster Scots people who might be considered untrustworthy, capricious or unpredictable. Perhaps it gets the odd outing

If a search were to be carried out in a slapdash manner, someone might be said to "hae a rummle through", perhaps equivalent to "rummage". However there is another meaning to "rummle through"; the sense of getting by, surviving, muddling through.

The Santy Clause

At Christmas... there is a strong possibility of visitors, either relatives (close or far oot) returned hame for the festive season, oul friends dropping by for a glass and a yarn or thon nuisance frae up (or down) the road stickin her neb in for nosiness. There is one visitor whose arrival is hotly anticipated by weans o aal ages, though younger yins in particular, and that's Santy.

A quare big boady (A doot he laiks his grub) wae a big white baird an whiskers, red coat an breeks, black well'tons an a red kep, he whiles haes a sled pullt by reindeer, but he's aye his loan when he comes doon yer chimley, loadened up wae presents, naw really carin whether ye wur naughty or nice. In me ain experience, Santy taks a brave an lenient view o' youthful misdemeanours an A'm gye an gled he daes or A'd get naethin or very little mesel.

This is a wee verse, writ for Christmas.

Santy's the boady tae bring youse yer toys
We see the weans wile joy again,
Weechils an cutties an hobbledehoys
Micht aiblins mine thon ither wean.

Hae yersels a guid yin an A hope Santy brings ye sumthin, whether ye wur naughty or nice. Wishing all a good Christmas.

Scunner and Lightning

There are a number of spellings; Jim Fenton has a preference for "scunther" and I have also come across "scunder" but for me, it's "scunner". It's both a noun and a verb; as a noun, it can mean an irrational dislike bordering on loathing or to feel or show disgust to a person or thing ("She tuk a wile scunner tae him"), as a verb it means to disgust, to nauseate, to take an aversion to someone or something ("He scunnered me").

If a person or object is obnoxious, either by nature, by behaviour or by personal hygiene, they can be classified as a "scunner" ("Wae his smart mooth an big heid, he's naethin but a scunner"; "The steuch risin aff him would a scunnered ye"; "A had that big a feed o' drink at Christmas an New Year, A'm clean scunnered wae the stuff") although the last might be classified as an extreme overreaction.

It is possible to take a scunner or even the scunners with a particular subject, either based on rational grounds although one can take the scunner (or scunners) on a whim.

The origin is Middle English and Scots but it is widely used in Scots and as such, can be found emblazoned on mugs, badges and tea towels frae Gretna Green tae Galloway an Glasgow.

There that mony o' them it would clean scunner ye.

Warm in the Shade

I note that one of the best-selling books of recent times is a volume called "50 Shades of Grey". While I am not totally sure to what extent this book will appeal to Ulster Scots, there is a very real danger that some of the sales in Ulster Scots speaking areas may be due to a fundamental misunderstanding of the word "shade". A "shade" in Ulster Scots is related to some meanings of the Standard English word "shed" but should not necessarily be regarded as an interchangeable substitute, certainly not in the sense of a garden shed.

A shade is a rude agricultural erection with a roof but not necessarily four walls. It shares the principle of the garden shed but not the design. Meant primarily for the storage of hay, straw or peat, the open architecture provides shelter from the elements for the contents while at the same time allowing for drying over time, a highly desirable outcome for peats, straw and hay.

There is a strong possibility that the Ulster Scot, when confronted with the title "50 Shades of Grey", might think this a volume dedicated to Mr. Grey's large number of agricultural storage structures, a celebration of his numerous rural repositories. This would be a misunderstanding which might bring a bright red blush to the cheek of an Ulster Scot.

Sham On You

I have often remarked on the extra value extracted from Standard English words by Ulster Scots. This is not only reflective of the innate thriftiness of our nature but also a tribute to our imagination and creativity.

Which brings me to "sham". We share the Standard English meaning of "sham" meaning simulated, fake, bogus, dummy, feigned, spurious, false or imitation. Perhaps the most obvious example of this occurs on 13th July (calendar permitting) in the County Down where King Billy and King James re-enact the Battle of the Boyne most years at the Sham Fight at Scarva.

Language is littered with words which can convey intimacy or at least friendship (occasionally threat) between strangers. The Glaswegian might address you as "pal" (and not always in a pally way), the Londoner as "John", the Nottingham native might say "duck"; the Ulster Scot may be inclined to say "sham". "Sham" conveys the sense of "Hey you" or "mate". "Sham" would normally be employed in a friendly way but can, on occasion, be deployed in a less genial manner, the interpretation almost totally dependent on tone and context.
So listen sham, am aff.

Shire Yer Heid

That good Ulster Scots word "shire" has nothing to do with Bilbo Baggins and the other inhabitants of the "Shire" (cinematically at least, none other than that son of North Antrim, Broughshane-born James Nesbitt) as featured in "The Lord of the Rings" and "The Hobbit".

No linkage either to the Shires of Britain or the breed of heavy draft horses (such as the Clydesdale) named for their place of breeding, the Shire horses bred in the Shires.

No, our "shire" has two distinct but related meanings. In a practical sense, "shire" means the settling and clarifying of muddy or cloudy liquid, perhaps referring to liquids obtained from the process of distillation.

The metaphorical sense is to refresh or to rest, particularly in times of stress. A common cry from the harassed Ulster Scot is "Gie me peace and let me get ma heed shired", translating as "Allow me a moment to collect my thoughts, sharpen my focus and regain my composure".

This sentiment is usually expressed when voices are raised, when contradictory advice or opinions are offered at high decibel levels or when disputation starts to turn to argument bordering on quarrel. This is a surprisingly common occurrence among Ulster Scots given their predilection for and ability to "rise a row in an empy hoose".

Am away tae get me ain heed shired.

Skelp on the Erse

Although used in Scotland (and to a lesser extent in parts of the North of England), "skelp" is not only widely heard in Ulster Scots speaking areas but also in areas which wouldn't necessarily designate themselves as native speaking.

While there is obviously a lack of certainty (and a certain amount of argument) about the origin of the word, one theory suggests it comes from Scottish Gaelic "sgealb" meaning a thin strip of wood and given that the majority of uses apply to physical chastisement, there seems to be a logic to this.

It can be used as a verb meaning to slap or to smack ("I'll skelp him when I get the houl o' him"; I will physically discipline him when next we meet) or a noun meaning the individual elements of a "skelpin" (I gin her a guid skelp). A skelp is usually applied to the hindquarters (a skelp on the arse) and can be utilised in relation to a jockey in the final furlongs of a race applying the whip to a tardy nag, Jockey Club permitting, or in a domestic disciplinary sense such as the correction or chastisement of a cheeky or disobedient offspring (implement optional), European Convention on Human Rights permitting, of course.

There is another sense, that of making good speed ("He was goin at a quare skelp"; his speed was almost certainly in excess of the legal limit). And in the same context, an encouragement to a driver (or a jockey) to increase his pace might be "Skelp 'er on, ye boy ye".

Additionally a considerable amount of ground or land might be referred to as "a skelp o' grun" ("She left him a quare skelp o' grun in her will"; his inheritance of land was substantial).

Skitter Account

I have touched before on the preponderance of abusive terms in Ulster Scots and indeed the preference of Ulster Scots speakers for words of criticism. Some are more light-hearted than others and a good case in point is skitter.

There is, of course, the formal medical use of the word "skitter", to denote a looseness of the bowels (diarrhoea), derived from a condition associated with a swine disease, pig skitter.

Once a common inquiry by nursing staff in hospital, (Have your bowels moved?), I am reminded of a Joey Dunlop tale.

After a gas cylinder exploded at his caravan, Joey was rushed to hospital. As he recuperated, a passing nurse asked "Did your bowels move?" Replied Joey, "Bowels, cups, plates and saucers; everythin was blew tae scrivens;" (All my crockery was damaged).

Back to "skitter". If an item or incident were of a sufficiently disgusting or upsetting nature, it could be said to "gie ye the skitter". If it was a particularly distressing event, it just might "skitter the guts oot o ye". A person who is a skitter is a low level irritant, a pest, someone with the ability to aggravate, annoy or exasperate. It is often used in conjunction with other insults so it is possible to be a skitter but more often you come across ignorant skitters, lazy skitters, cheeky skitters and many other varieties of skitter. This is often applied in a jocular manner with little venom but nevertheless, it is not a compliment.

There is also an implication of insignificance, and can be a reference to the puny or inconsequential nature of an individual, such as "that wee skitter" or often "Come here, you wee skitter".

A light hearted Ulster Scots expression. Naw mony o them.

Slap Happy

The Australian cultural phenomenon "The Slap", a best-selling book and a hit international television series, brings to mind the Ulster Scots use of the word "slap".

Of course , we share the standard English (and Australian) meaning of a blow, a broad stroke made with the hand open or using the back of the hand, differing from a punch, made with a fist. Slaps can be made across the face, hands or any other body part, used in phrases like "a slap in the mooth" or "she hut him a quare slap on the erse".

However, the Ulster Scot also uses "slap" to denote an opening into a field (a big slap, a wee slap) and you might well "cap coos" (cows) (or for that matter, any farm animals) through a slap, i.e. direct cattle through an opening into a field.

I have heard it said that "capping cows" was a reference to the use of the (flat) cap as an aide to controlling and directing the beasts.
I have also heard this theory roundly derided.

Make your own mind up

Slip Sliding Away

With "slip", there is a broad sharing of meaning with Standard English but Ulster Scots, as usual, takes the raw material and bends it to the needs of the native speaker.

The Ulster Scot possessed of a sharp tongue (her tongue's that sharp, she'll laikly cut hersel) are rarely able to resist an opportunity to have a quick dig at someone or "slip yin in", as we say, rather like a metaphorical stiletto. "Slippy terms" is a description, usually a criticism, of a business arrangement such as a contract or a lease, any deal which has not been as clearly defined and negotiated as it might have been.

An untrustworthy individual, one without morals, scruples or ethics can best be described as a "slippy tit".

As a caution to those who may be getting ideas above their pay grade (an activity abhorred by all right thinking Ulster Scots), the fallibility of the human being can best be summed up in the phrase "there's a slippy stane ootside iveryboady's dour".

Totally unrelated but there's a tale told of a new parish priest arriving in the village and at confessions, many of the parishioners 'fessed up to marital infidelity and other shenanigans. However, Father didn't care for the graphic terms in which these actions were described so he told his congregation to refer to these activities as "slipping".

Years passed and a new young priest arrived in the parish. He walked out of the church where he met a roadsweeper (a surfaceman to those of a certain age). "There must be terrible litter in this village because nearly everybody at confession has been slipping everywhere". The roadsweeper roared with laughter. The priest looked at him, "I don't know what you're laughing at, your own wife has slipped three times this week. If this carries on, she's likely to break her leg".

Laik I toul yes, a slippy stane ootside iveryboady's dour.

Naw mine, of coorse.

No Targe

Anyone familiar with Ulster Scots will be aware of the Tongue's propensity for terms of abuse and the shortage of words of praise. This is partly a reflection of the environment, partly to do with the people, both quite unforgiving. There is also a rich strand of Ulster Scots dedicated to the war of the sexes, the unflagging, unforgiving struggle between men and weemin, whether within the noble estate of matrimony or outside.

Which brings us to, "targe", a quite harsh assessment of an assertive female, particularly one who is unafraid to share some positive criticism of men, either in general or in particular.

A female who is keen to offer helpful advice to the male of the species, whether in the context of a personal relationship or a professional one, or perhaps within the local community, is poorly regarded in the world of Ulster Scots. The term "targe" is an insult rarely used in the presence of the said "targe" but is rather uttered behind their back, not a particularly manly action but one which proves the truism "she's mair o'a man than you'll ever be".

The Ulster Scots male takes criticism not well and is inclined to berate the critic rather than take notice of any shortcomings or flaws identified by the "targe".

There is an infinitesimally small chance that male behaviour may draw some tiny measure of censure from their significant female other, possibly relating to the misuse, or indeed overuse, of alcoholic beverages. The clever ones will say nothing that night, like a friend of mine whose husband was wont to roll home "full as a po".

"I never mention any thing to him when he comes home" she told me. I asked why.

"He's too drunk" she replied, "I wait till morning and his head is thumping and his stomach churning, then I give him what for".
I'm sure you'll agree, she's a bit of a targe.
Go easy on the fallin doon water.

Thole on Ice

One of the qualities I treasure most in the Ulster Scots is the ability to endure, to bear, to suffer, to tolerate, the ability to "thole".

I remember being in pain as a wean (youngster) due to getting a skelf, a splinter of wood, stuck just below the skin. By the way, a skelf can also be used to describe a small thin person, an undernourished individual, an unhealthily slim soul, a small, perhaps an insignificant, person.

Anyway, back to the wooden skelf, the remedy involves the application of a needle or other sharp implement to gouge out the offending fragment from under your skin. Hard as it may be to believe, this is not as pleasant an experience as it sounds and the sight of an approaching adult with a sharpened sliver of steel with which to poke around in your flesh can be upsetting to a younger person.

"Houl still" I was encouraged. "Quet cryin" I was instructed. "Just thole a wee bit" I was told.

In my memory, the skelf was eventually dislodged by the tidal wave of blood released from the wound but it may not have been as dramatic as that.

Despite the bitter salt tears of youth, like a lot of Ulster Sots, I got better at the tholin as the years passed.

And it wasn't always pain that had to be tholed. Provocation could also be tholed ("I had tae listen that much oul guff frae him I cud hardy thole it"; His rantings were almost too difficult to endure).

A tiresome individual, a bore or a blowhard or just a loud person can be hard tae thole. For some people, there can be a problem with the success or good fortune of others (especially when compared to one's own lack of such talent or luck) which may make it tough tae thole.

The highest praise available is to be described as a "tholer", someone fit to suffer the slings and arrows of outrageous fortune with equanimity and stoicism.

I am sure an' certain yes hae tholed enough o' this.

A Thong at Twilight

Thong has an existing Standard English meaning, or at least a fairly recently added meaning, that is a brief undergarment for the lower body that exposes the buttocks (or erse, as we say in Ulster Scots), consisting of a strip of fabric passing between the thighs and attached to a band around the waist.

Needless to say, given the inclement weather in Ulster, this type of underwear was not a popular choice for the average Ulster Scots lassy, or so I am assured by my weemin freens who were all uniformly clad in serge bloomers.

So they tell me.

The Ulster Scots meaning of 'thong' harks back to an earlier Standard English one, a thin strip of leather or a whip.

If an individual's behaviour was considered beyond the pale, it was inevitably concluded that "He didnae get near thonged enough when he was a wean", perhaps an Ulster Scots version of "Spare the rod and spoil the child".

And of coorse, a thongin was usually delivered by whatever article was to hand rather than the whip which use of the word might imply. In matters of corporal punishment, the Ulster Scot is nothing if not fond of improvisation.

If someone "played thong", this carried no hint of impropriety involving scanty panties but rather meant that someone had lashed out, whether with a whip or without, both are equally possible. This was sometimes rendered as "played swipe".

And to receive a thongin was to be on the wrong end of a damned good thrashing.

Am aff tae continue my research intae the popularity o' serge bloomers amang Ulster Scots weemin.
If A get a thongin', ye'll know what happened.

Yock an Roll

One of the difficulties with Ulster Scots is that it, in the main, doesn't lend itself to a process of read-across translation. This is not an immutable rule and there are plenty of examples thrown up of words with shared meanings but slightly different spellings and significantly different pronunciations.

"Yock" comes pretty close in meaning to the Standard English "yoke", a device used for joining or attaching working animals to farm implements such as ploughs, harrows or carts.

Like a good jazz player, the Ulster Scot can take that reasonably straightforward definition and improvise away to their heart's content, creating new, different meanings, often with little or no relationship to the original.

An encouragement to a tardy worker engaged with attaching a tractor to a trailer or a horse to a plough, or a husband hitching the caravan to a car, might be told to "Get 'er yocked!".

After the yockin has been completed and the driver takes to the road, if the speed of travel is less than that desired by a passenger (or a spouse), an encouragement to speed up is "Yock 'er on".

I have heard folk comment on an odd-looking vehicle or machine (think of Heath Robinson or Rube Goldberg contraption) with the remark "Ye should a seen the yock he was drivin" or "He turned up in a quare yock o' a thing".

Closer to the original meaning is the comment on the mature marriage, where both participants are considered old enough and hence wise enough to know better; "They're yockin when they should be lowsin"; they are tying a knot when they really should be loosening it.

Occasionally I have come across "yock" being used when referring to the yellow part of an egg, the yolk.

I feel I can now consider mesel well an truly "unyocked".